ABOUT CANADA
QUEER RIGHTS

Peter Knegt

About Canada Series

Fernwood Publishing • Halifax & Winnipeg

Editing: Ruth Bradley-St-Cyr
Cover design: John van der Woude
Printed and bound in Canada by Hignell Book Printing

Published in Canada by Fernwood Publishing
32 Oceanvista Lane, Black Point, Nova Scotia, B0J 1B0
and 748 Broadway Avenue, Winnipeg, MB R3G 0X3
www.fernwoodpublishing.ca

Fernwood Publishing Company Limited gratefully acknowledges the financial support of the Government of Canada through the Canada Book Fund, the Canada Council for the Arts, the Nova Scotia Department of Tourism and Culture, the Manitoba Department of Culture, Heritage and Tourism under the Manitoba Publishers Marketing Assistance Program and the Province of Manitoba, through the Book Publishing Tax Credit, for our publishing program.

Library and Archives Canada Cataloguing in Publication

Knegt, Peter, 1984-
About Canada : queer rights / Peter Knegt.

(About Canada)
Includes bibliographical references.
ISBN 978-1-55266-456-8 (bound).–ISBN 978-1-55266-437-7 (pbk.)

1. Gay rights–Canada–History. 2. Gays–Canada–Social conditions.
3. Homosexuality–Canada–History. I. Title. II. Series: About Canada series

HQ76.3.C3K64 2011   323.3'2640971   C2011-903219-8

CONTENTS

1. WHAT DOES OUR PROGRESS MEAN?

Canada is often regarded as a country that is highly evolved in acknowledging the rights of queer people. The American media, for example, often refer to Canada as a "queer utopia," especially relative to themselves. This perception is largely due to the 2005 federal legalization of same-sex marriage, making Canada the fourth country in the world, and the first in the Western hemisphere, to do so. With that milestone, many assumed that an "end of law" had been reached for queer Canadians in reforming the legal system. We had also certainly managed to outpace our southern neighbours, who continue to struggle in doing the same.

But is our queer-friendly designation justified? Canada is indeed one of the most progressive countries in the world when it comes to the formal rights of queer people. Officially, we enjoy nearly all of the same legal rights as our heterosexual counterparts, from marriage and adoption to access to housing and employment. But some crucial factors need to be kept in mind when considering Canada's reputation: first, that this has not always been the case. Young people — queer or otherwise — are likely aware of this simple fact, but likely much less aware of the specifics. Such as how the 1965 arrest of a mechanic in the Northwest Territories triggered the partial decriminalization of homosexuality four years later. Or how, in 1981, police violently raided a series of gay establishments in Toronto, resulting both in one of the largest mass arrests in Canadian history and, shortly thereafter, the largest demonstration for lesbian and gay rights in that same history. Or how, in 1989, a group of AIDS activists stormed the International Conference on AIDS in Montreal, stealing the stage from Prime Minister Brian Mulroney to protest his government's ignorance of how AIDS was affecting gay and bisexual men. The examples are countless and each offers a glimpse of the pervasive system of formal and informal sanctions and persecutions that have challenged queer Canadians. They also offer a better understanding of the climate we exist in today.

"Examining historical experiences and practices can help us understand from where lesbian and gay oppression and, more generally, oppressive sexual regulation has come, where it may be going, and the possibilities for transformation," Gary Kinsman writes in *The Regulation of Desire: Homo and Hetero Sexualities*, one of the foremost studies regarding the history of Canadian sexuality.[1] By looking at some of the key events and processes, we can historicize queer issues in Canada, thereby gaining comprehension of the present. Certainly this will highlight the fact that in a relatively short period of time, queer activism and advocacy have achieved extraordinary goals. But it's also important to ask what exactly these changes mean, especially the public policy and law reforms, such as same-sex marriage. To the extent that there has been change, how deep are those changes and how diverse are the constituencies affected by them? This is really the core question about this history.

Many people writing on queer issues in Canada dispute the significance of the official progress made in terms of actual social change. Gary Kinsman, for example, argues that many queer people have been regulated and normalized by all these legal victories.[2] This observation stems from the ideology of lesbian and gay liberation, which was the bold, militant movement born in the early 1970s that spearheaded the fight for the rights of queer people in this country. Tom Warner, another leading voice on the subject, defines the impetus of the gay and lesbian liberation movement as the "products of anger and outrage channelled into collective action." Fundamentally, it was about changing self-image. "Changing a few laws and achieving tolerance are necessary, but insufficient in themselves to achieve fundamental social change," Warner writes in *Never Going Back: A History of Queer Activism in Canada*. "At the risk of oversimplification, lesbian and gay liberation may be summed up as a revolutionary struggle that seeks the eradication of heterosexism and the overthrow of the dictatorship of compulsory heterosexuality."[3]

Liberation activism was gradually surpassed by a more conservative, assimilationist advocacy fighting for legal recognition of same-sex relationships. While on one end of the spectrum, some argue that this achievement does not coincide with what gay and lesbian liberationists originally intended, others argue that drastic changes in public opinion toward queer people prove that these victories have indeed brought forth significant societal acceptance. But most can agree that there are drastic variations in progress and privileges across the "queer spectrum." One of the defining features of Canada's queer community is also one of the principal characteristics of Canada itself: remarkable diversity is found under this umbrella. Spread across different cultural regions and co-defined by a variety of races, ethnicities, classes and belief systems, Canada's queer community is not easily generalized and is not particularly equal either. Same-sex marriage, for example, is not an "end law" and certainly not an "end issue" for a large portion of Canadian queers. The term "queer," it should be clarified, refers to all non-heterosexual people. In most cases, "queer" ends up being shorthand for "gay or lesbian," which are the identity groups primarily discussed in this book. However, the word is intentionally more inclusive and ambiguous, as further explained in Chapter 7. Gays and lesbians are not alone in experiencing the two overarching and inter-connected problems of homophobia and heterosexism.

In the 1970s, the term "homophobia" was adopted as "the preferred term to describe the cause of the oppression of and discrimination against homosexuals."[4] In a 1975 leaflet distributed by the lesbian and gay liberation group Gays of Ottawa, homophobia was described as follows:

> Homophobia like other kinds of prejudice — racism, sexism — manifests itself in many ways… Today there is a whole gamut of homophobic reactions — outright queer-bashing, psychiatry's attempts to 'cure' the homosexual, discriminatory laws and employment practices, inability on the part of social service agencies to deal with the homosexual, the media's demeaning and stereotypical images of the homosexual, pseudo-liberalism's tolerance of the homosexual so long as she or he remains invisible — all reactions from a combination of ignorance and fear.[5]

As this description suggests, homophobia can manifest itself in many ways. Individualized homophobia refers to one individual's belief that homosexuality is wrong or immoral and, at its extreme, can result in verbal or physical abuse. However, this book focuses instead on institutional homophobia and thus provides an analysis of broad social relations in Canadian society. Institutional homophobia, which refers to various institutions discriminating against people because of their sexuality, is largely outlawed thanks to the *Canadian Charter of Rights and Freedoms* but is far from eradicated. Having legislation to protect queer people from discrimination is one thing, but changing the heterosexist ideologies that drive the institutions — and the individuals behind them — is quite another.

Heterosexism is a complex term described by Tom Warner as not simply the manifestation of ignorance and fear, but also of "the power wielded by the state and by social and commercial institutions that systematically promote, tolerate, or sanction prejudice."[6] Essentially, it is the social system that favours opposite-sex sexuality and relationships, including the presumption that everyone is heterosexual or that heterosexual attraction and relationships are "normal" and therefore superior. Gary Kinsman prefers to frame his noted work *The Regulation of Desire* around heterosexism, explaining that homophobia can be seen "as a particularly virulent personal response organized by heterosexist discourse and practice." He sees heterosexism as relating the practices of heterosexual hegemony to "institutional and social settings and to sex and gender relations without reducing gay and lesbian oppression to an 'effect' of gender."[7] Either way, these interrelated effects of heterosexism and institutionalized homophobia are dominant villains in the queer Canadian history narrative and remain intensely active today, affecting a wide range of issues, including censorship, the *Criminal Code*, the education system, the health industry, the media, and the emotional and physical harassment of queer people, which sometimes turns violent.

That is why it is important not only to understand the history of queer Canada, but also to utilize that understanding to look past the myth of a "queer utopia" that same-sex marriage has perpetrated. This is the mandate of this book. While momentous strides have certainly been made, today's society is not the result that gay and lesbian liberationists — the people who started Canada's queer rights movement — envisioned. The "overthrow of the dictatorship of compulsory heterosexuality" has not occurred. If anything, same-sex marriage has seen privileged lesbians and gays assimilate into the norms of this dictatorship, leaving behind their queer comrades who can't participate because their lifestyles do not "fit" into mainstream society.

We must keep in mind that the purpose of this book is *not* to create an encyclopedic and inclusive detailing of Canadian queer people. We are a vast and complex bunch, with thousands and thousands of fascinating stories, pivotal figures, hard fought victories and unjust losses. It is impossible to fairly chronicle in a book of this length, or perhaps even one fifty times longer, this entire rich and complex history. What this book *will* do is introduce a history that is widely misunderstood and widely underreported, and then provide direction to continue that educational journey. Books by noted writers like Gary Kinsman and Tom Warner, as well as works by Dionne Brand, Line

Chamberland, Elise Chenier, Brenda Cossman, Ross Higgins, Bruce MacDougall, Steven Maynard, Donald McLeod, David Rayside, Michael Riordan, Becki L. Ross, Makeda Silvera, George Smith, Miriam Smith, Rinaldo Walcott and Thomas Waugh, among others, collectively provide an exhaustive schooling on queer Canada. As do the many human resources we may not realize surround us. Oral histories remain one of the most effective ways to learn, and it was largely through them that this book came together.

Unlike many of the aforementioned authors, I am not writing from first-hand experience. Instead, this book comes from the enlightenment provided by those very authors, as well as from a variety of other resources, like the 135 issues of the *Body Politic*, Canada's pre-eminent gay and lesbian liberation magazine, or the exhaustive website of late queer activist Rick Bebout, chronicling both his own life and the queer history that surrounded it.[8] And from dozens of queer Canadians themselves, who offered their time and their stories to illuminate the intricacy of our shared history, a history I admit was not as well known to me as I had once assumed. As a white, middle-class, gay male who entered my twenties as same-sex marriage was being passed into legislation, the experience of writing this book made it all the more clear how easily social privilege can produce ignorance. Thus the primary goal of *About Canada: Queer Rights* is to provide the first step forward for readers to become aware both of how one of Canada's greatest social movements came to be, and of how much work is left to be done.

2. REGIONAL ORGANIZING

Before this book explores more specific aspects of Canadian queer history, it is useful to provide a brief snapshot of how the community first formed. As noted in the previous chapter, lesbian and gay liberation, originating in the early 1970s, was the activism that spearheaded over a decade of remarkably valiant efforts in fighting for the human rights of queer people (though at that point, and largely still today, it was very much about lesbians and gays, as will be made clear). Emerging in a context of revolution and civil rights for women, blacks, First Nations, Quebecois and youth, lesbian and gay liberation brought forceful, active organization that drastically changed the way many queer Canadians live their lives. This is not to say that such activism did not occur before this period. Queer Canadians have existed as long as the country has, and forms of activism have existed along with them (for example, see the story of Canada's first gay activist, James Egan). More officially, though, it was in the mid- to late-1960s when the first "homophile organizations" emerged that the country's true beginnings in terms of organizing occurred. These groups were influenced by events in the United States since the 1950s (oddly enough, much of Canada's earliest organizing was modelled after their southern neighbours, despite the current assumption that Canada is much more advanced than the U.S. in terms of queer rights). They were largely dedicated to educating both the public and homosexuals themselves toward a greater acceptance of homosexuality. But while their efforts were imperative, the flawed and relatively short-lived movement was overtaken by lesbian and gay liberation in the early 1970s. By the mid-1980s, much of the attention that the movement was devoting to the fight for human rights was sidetracked by the advent of HIV/AIDS, discussed in detail in Chapter 6. By the 1990s, for a variety of reasons, including the emotional and financial exhaustion of activist groups and the advent of a more assimilationist objective that was a driving force behind the legalization of same-sex marriage, the presence of lesbian and gay liberation declined. It certainly did not disappear, but its most influential period had clearly passed.

It is crucial to understand, though, that essentially every right that has come to queer Canadians is at least partially the result of this initial organization of Canada's queer community; however, paradoxically, it is also questionable even to consider such a thing as a "Canadian queer community." The many identities within the spectrum rarely come together as one "community" socially, and even less so politically (more on that in Chapter 7), and moreover, there is simply too much regional variation in this country for one coherent narrative to represent the entire Canadian queer movement. This is true of a wide variety of Canadian histories, largely because the country has a small population distributed in clumps across a vast geography. So in telling this very condensed version of Canada's queer activist origins, it seems only fair to do so from a variety of geographic points of view. Besides, that's truly how Canada's queer organizing began. It did not begin as some great national movement and then filter down to the local level. It started with a few dozen movements in a few dozen communities, some more influential than others, but all crucial in their own right.

British Columbia

Despite being much smaller in population than Toronto and Montreal, Vancouver — the clear centre of British Columbia's queer community — played a considerable role in the earliest days of activist organizing. Largely influenced by its proximity to similar groups in California, Vancouver was the home of Canada's first and most successful "homophile organization," the Association for Social Knowledge (ASK), founded in April 1964. The specific ambition of ASK was "to seriously confront Canadian society with the fact of its homosexual minority and challenge Canadians to treat homosexuals with justice and respect and to work for reform of criminal laws on social activity."[1] They relied heavily on experts like psychiatrists and doctors and were committed to the "adjustment" of homosexuals into society. Though they had dissolved by 1969, ASK played a considerable role in the decriminalization of homosexuality.[2]

Lesbian and gay liberation also came to Canada by way of Vancouver in the form of the Gay Liberation Front (GLF), an activist, communal collective to combat gay oppression, which formed in November 1970. It did not prove as enduring as ASK, and was succeeded by the Gay Alliance Toward Equality (GATE) the following May. GATE was one of the first Canadian groups to plan civil rights strategies. It was also known for its "no-compromise positions, several of which were adopted as policy and for discussion by the Canadian gay movement."[3] GATE would prove active and quite influential until 1980 (a lengthy life for a gay organization at the time), and it would be instrumental in forming the National Gay Election Coalition, which brought together sixteen groups from across the country to intervene in the 1972 federal election. The group also organized Vancouver's first Pride celebrations in 1973, holding a picnic and art exhibit in Ceperley Park, and brought the very first queer rights case to the Supreme Court of Canada when the publication *Gay Tide* submitted a classified advertisement to the *Vancouver Sun* that the newspaper refused to publish because they felt readers "would find it offensive."[4] The proposed ad simply read, "Subs. to *Gay Tide*, Gay Lib Paper. 6 monthly issues. $1. Box 6572. Station G, Van 8." GATE sued the newspaper for discrimination, but ultimately lost.

As in every other major Canadian city, police harassment of gays and lesbians in Vancouver was a serious problem. It grew so excessive by the mid-1970s that groups began picketing police stations and asked the municipal government to intervene. Recommendations concerning the treatment of gay clubs and bars by police, licensing and inspection officers and other city officials were presented to city council by the Standing Committee on Social Services. Many activists did not feel these recommendations properly addressed the homophobia within these institutions, and by 1977, police harassment was again in full force. In the first four months of the year, over 100 gay men were entrapped and arrested by plainclothes police in Vancouver on moral charges, leading to a large-scale protest at a public meeting called by police to discuss "prostitutes and other unsavory characters."[5]

Early organizing was not exclusive to Vancouver. Victoria saw the Gay People's Alliance form in April 1974 to promote lesbian and gay "pride, equality and liberation" in the city, but it had collapsed by that autumn.

No discussion of British Columbia's queer history would be complete without mention of Little Sister's Book and Art Emporium, Vancouver's gay and lesbian bookstore that opened in 1983. Though it falls outside the chronology discussed in this chapter, the store's legal battle against harassment from Canada Customs — which began in the mid-1980s and continued through December 2000 — is crucial in the history of censorship in Canada and was a defining battle for British Columbia's queer community.

Alberta and the Prairies

There was perhaps more collaboration among the trio of urban areas that were clear leaders in western Canadian activism than between any other communities in the country. Lesbian and gay liberation organizations in Winnipeg, Saskatoon and Edmonton held conferences for Prairie activists in the 1970s that discussed the movement, funding, counselling and community relations. Individually, each community made its mark as its respective province's centre of activity. Their organizing occurred on a much smaller scale than in Vancouver, Montreal and Toronto, but was no less important to the lives of the people it brought together.

The first liberation organization in Alberta was the Gay Alliance Toward Equality Edmonton (GATE-Edmonton), which started in 1971. Some of the group's early activities were lobbying the Alberta government to amend the *Alberta Bill of Rights* and the *Individual's Rights Protection Act* to outlaw discrimination based on sexual orientation (which would not come to fruition until the late 1990s).

Edmonton's community was greatly affected by the maliciousness of the local police force, most notably when police raided the Pisces Spa — a gay men's bathhouse — in 1981, arresting sixty men as "keepers or found-ins in a common bawdyhouse." GATE-Edmonton organized leafleting of bars within twenty-four hours, resulting in a hundred people demonstrating in front of city hall to protest the raid. Michael Phair, an Edmonton gay activist who would become the city's first openly gay city counsellor and an influential figure in the city's queer history, explained that the effect of the incident on the community was sizable. "I think before [the raid] much of what was being done on a political level was being done by a relatively small number of people," he said. "The rest thought perhaps it was better to stay under the radar. But that incident changed that quite dramatically."[6]

Saskatoon's activist community launched officially in April 1971 when Gay Alliance Toward Equality Saskatoon (GATE-Saskatoon) formed as a small group devoted to liberation. Later that year, the Gay Students Alliance (GSA) was organized at the city's University of Saskatchewan, which would lead to creation of the Zodiac Friendship Society (known as the Saskatoon Gay Community Centre after 1975), an organization coordinating social services and activities in the gay community. That group opened one of the country's biggest gay community centres, right downtown in Saskatoon on a busy street. The groups in Saskatoon had many other stories. They set a precedent for the Canadian movement in 1973 when they obtained a pro-gay statement from the Saskatchewan Human Rights Commission and launched the famous case around Doug Wilson.

Winnipeg's first gay and lesbian organization was the Happenings Club, a social centre that opened in 1971. The club had 743 members by June 1975.[7] Winnipeg would see its first gay political organization, Gays For Equality (GFE) formed by students at the University of Manitoba in 1972. The group's first major project was organizing Winnipeg's first Gay Pride Week. The Winnipeg community also made an important contribution to Canadian gay history with the twenty-four-page newsprint booklet *Understanding Homosexuality*, published in the mid-1970s. Containing excerpts from academic research and religious publications, it was aimed at people working in professional social services. An initial attempt at publication saw the printing company refuse to print the book because it presented homosexuality favourably.

Relatively, the Prairies' other major urban areas — Regina and Calgary — had much less political activity. "Regina was basically nothing but a bar," long-time Saskatchewan-based activist Gens Hellquist said.[8] In 1973, a queer political group tried to form at the University of Saskatchewan's Regina campus but had difficulty finding members.

Calgary had and still has a much more complex situation. Its gay community had a definite presence socially, with bars and social clubs comparable to that of Edmonton, but was always challenged politically. Though the city's activist group Gay Information and Resources Calgary formed in 1976, Stephen Lock, one of the city's most prominent early activists, noted that the community tended to be generally apolitical when it came to queer rights and continues to be somewhat "behind the times."[9] This may be a reaction to the social and political environment in which queer Calgarians — and Albertans — exist. There is substantial truth to the mythology surrounding Alberta regarding its reputation as Canada's most heterosexist and institutionally homophobic province, as will be made clear. The Alberta government has resisted extending human rights protections to sexual minorities more than any other province. While Edmonton has benefited from a relatively progressive civil government, Calgary's community continues to face one of the more hostile situations for urban queer Canadians. As recently as the mid-2000s, the city saw a series of bathhouse raids by the Calgary Police Service. In 2007, then-mayor Dave Bronconnier publicly said he could not condone the "gay lifestyle" when Tourism Calgary began promoting the city as a queer travel destination.[10]

Ontario

Ontario's gay and lesbian movement — and much literature about it — has certainly centred on Toronto, but there have been notable movements in communities across the province. London, Waterloo and Guelph all began gay groups through their local universities in 1971, not long after Toronto had established its first groups. London actually had the largest gay community centre in Canada when the Homophile Association of London opened its 10,000 square foot headquarters in 1974.[11] By the end of the decade, gay and lesbian organizations had also formed in Thunder Bay, Windsor, Hamilton, Mississauga, Peterborough, Kingston and, most significantly, Ottawa.

Ottawa formed an organization to lobby the federal and provincial governments on behalf of gays and lesbians in 1971, and work as a community organization for gays and lesbians in the area. Adopting the name Gays of Ottawa/Gays d'Ottawa (GO), the group was one of the most important lesbian and gay activist organizations in the early days of the movement. Distinctive in its bilingualism, GO played a large role in organizing around national issues. They also launched a public campaign to press for the protection of lesbians

James Egan: Canada's First Gay Activist

"I cannot understand why so many men spend years, sometimes even a lifetime, agonizing over the fact that they're gay. I never felt the need for society's permission or approval to live my life." —Jim Egan

In 1949, being openly gay in Canada seemed impossible. Even in the biggest cities, there were no clubs or support groups, nor much evidence of any sort of community. Moreover, there was a serious risk of being thrown in jail for years and declared a "dangerous sexual offender" simply for being homosexual. But in 1949 — some twenty years before Canada's *Criminal Code* partially decriminalized homosexual acts — Jim Egan somehow managed to become the country's first known public gay activist.

Living in and around Toronto, Egan began his activist career quite simply by writing countless letters to editors of magazines and newspapers that had printed ridiculously ignorant and homophobic articles. Though the vast majority of his letters went unpublished, they sparked a passion in Egan, and led him to write a series of articles for Toronto's *True New Times* called "Aspects of Homosexuality" in late 1951. These were the first articles published in Canada from a gay point of view, and Egan would go on to write similar articles for a variety of publications through the 1950s.

In the 1960s, Egan's continued writings made him a very rare public gay figure, which ostracized him from much of the gay community, many of whom questioned or feared the awareness of homosexuality that he was promoting. At that time, ironically, homophobia was actually less of a problem because few people in mainstream society were aware that such a thing as homosexuality even existed. His activism also proved problematic to his relationship with his long-time lover, Jack Nesbit, which became strained from all the attention Egan was receiving (and because the couple's phone had in effect become a gay crisis line). So in 1964, Egan decided to give up activism and move with Nesbit to rural British Columbia.

After twenty years of reclusivity, both Egan and Nesbit again became well-known gay public figures. In 1987, they decided to use the *Canadian Charter of Rights and Freedoms* to challenge the exclusion of pension benefits to same-sex couples under the *Old Age Security Act*. In 1994, after nearly eight years of unsuccessful hearings and appeals, it became the first claim involving gay rights ever heard in the

Supreme Court of Canada under the *Charter*. The result was bittersweet: they lost the case, five votes to four, but at the same time, the Supreme Court ruled that the equality rights section of the *Charter* should now be read to include sexual orientation. This had a massive influence on the future of queer rights in Canada.

Because of the case, Egan and Nesbit's story was told in numerous newspaper and magazine articles, on television programs, and eventually in the documentary "Jim Loves Jack." In 1998, the pair celebrated their 50th anniversary.

Learn More: *Challenging the Conspiracy of Silence: My Life as a Canadian Gay Activist,* Jim Egan, compiled and edited by Donald W. McLeod (Toronto: The Canadian Gay and Lesbian Archives and Homewood Books, 1998).

and gay men under the Canadian Human Rights Commission, proposed in Bill C-72 in 1975.

One of the defining events in Ottawa came in 1975 when sixteen clients of a "male modelling agency" were arrested and charged in connection with a so-called "prostitution ring" in Ottawa. Local newspapers — with the cooperation of police — listed the names of all the men arrested. This resulted in nine of the men losing their jobs, and one of them committing suicide.[12] GO picketed the police station and the office of the *Ottawa Journal* to protest the arrests and the media coverage. This was a clear example of the mainstream media igniting homophobic moral panic, a classic narrative in the history of queer people in Canada.

As for Toronto, the city has a queer history that could fill dozens of books. Its organizing began with the University of Toronto Homophile Association (UTHA) — the first gay university organization in Canada and one of the first homophile organizations in Ontario — formed in October 1969. Out of UTHA would "spin off" the Community Homophile Association of Toronto (CHAT), created in December 1970 after the university group became overwhelmed with people from the general community. George Hislop — a prominent public figure in the city's queer history who ran for city council in 1980 in an election plagued by homophobic campaigning — was the group's first director. CHAT helped put together Toronto's first "gay picnic" on August 1, 1971, on Toronto Island, where 300 people attended, waving flags and banners. The following year, it became known as Gay Pride Week, which Mayor William Dennison refused to declare officially.

In 1972, many members of CHAT resigned due to the organization's "limiting structures and conservative goals," many of them becoming figures in the Gay Alliance Toward Equality (GATE), Toronto's first major lesbian and gay liberation group.[13] Organized by writers of the Toronto-based liberation magazine the *Body Politic* — a hugely influential institution in itself — this group lasted until 1980, and proved a major force in lesbian and gay liberation. CHAT would continue as well, and the two groups, which had very different ideologies, often came into conflict when concurrently taking up certain issues.

An iconic event in the Toronto community's history came in 1981, when the city faced a massive, violent raid on four bathhouses resulting in the arrest of 304 men. It was one of the largest mass arrests in Canadian history, and came after a series of smaller but no less terrifying campaigns by Toronto police. George Hislop was quoted in the *Body Politic* as calling the night "the gay equivalent of Crystal Night in Nazi Germany — when the Jews found out where they were really at."[14] By the following evening, activists had already organized a demonstration, showing unprecedented community mobilization as more than 3000 people marched toward Toronto's 52 Division police station chanting "Fuck You 52!"[15]

"That was a really pivotal moment because prior to 1981, there'd been little groups of gay liberationists… around the *Body Politic* and around Gay Alliance Toward Equality or around other organizations," long-time Toronto queer activist Tim McCaskell said, echoing the results on the gay community of the aforementioned Edmonton example. "But we were generally pretty isolated. The kinds of people that went out to bars and baths kind of thought we were off the wall. And I think there was a kind of arrogance that we were 'the enlightened, liberated ones' and then these were people living kind of half in, half out of the closet. But what the bathhouse raids did was to bring those groups together. They were such an attack on mainstream, ordinary gay men and produced such visceral anger."[16] What resulted from the raids was that "ordinary" gay men, people who owned small businesses in the community and many "ordinary" lesbians, all outraged by what was occurring, began to take part in action. Suddenly, everyone was on the same page.[17]

Quebec

As with most "Canadian histories," it's obvious that the situation for Quebec is quite particular. But defining that particularity — especially in a few pages — is rather difficult.[18]

In a December 1976 article in the *Body Politic*, Ron Dayman analyzed the first half-decade of the "the Quebec gay movement," which he explains is essentially limited to Montreal and Quebec City.[19] Dayman's article noted that if solidarity had been a major focus of the Canadian movement, "one must say that the history of the Quebec gay movement has been one of division and polarities." Two of these predominate: a linguistic and cultural polarity, and a polarity of ideologies. These polarities are not restricted to the gay movement, but are social realities of Quebec itself.

Quebec City's community was less divided than Montreal's, as it was less culturally and linguistically diverse, but it was certainly not without its disunity. Its first group, Centre humanitaire d'aide et de libération (CHAL), was formed in May 1973. A social service and organizing centre for gay men and lesbians, the group also held the first pan-Canadian gay and lesbian conference in October 1973, with eighty delegates attending from across the country. Interestingly, CHAL had particularly close ties with Arcadie, a very similar Paris-based French homophile organization. Like many other groups, CHAL eventually became divided between its conservative and progressive members, with the latter eventually leaving the group and having difficulty organizing themselves thereafter. This in turn saw CHAL gradually become more of a service organization than an activist group.

Montreal's early organizing is a clearer example of Dayman's noted polarities. "Anglophone groups kind of held the field in the beginning, but there were Francophones working in those groups," Ross Higgins of the Archives gai du Québec said of Montreal. "In the mid-1970s when all of the action started, the emphasis swung back to Francophone organizing. And for the most part that was the dominant pattern from that point forward. Organizing Anglophones seemed a very enclosed and ghettoized activity in many ways."[20]

The first Francophone gay organization, the Front de libération homosexuelle (FLH), was formed in 1971. The organization was said to have attracted "a wide diversity of men and women with differing goals and ideologies."[21] By the end of the year, however, the story once again saw more progressive members (including its founders) leave the group when it decided to incorporate legally and focus more on being service-oriented and social. Attempts to open a service centre were met with raids by the police, leading to many members being scared away and the group collapsing by the autumn of 1972.

The first Anglophone organization came the same year, with GAY (later Gay McGill), forming through McGill University. The group emerged out of a popular course at McGill called "Biology and Social Change" that discussed gay-consciousness. Notable were the dances held from 1973 to 1974, which were estimated to be the most popular regularly held gay dances in the world, attracting more than 2000 people.[22] The Quebec liquor permit board refused to renew the group's liquor licence in April 1975, which led to the end of the dances. In the meantime, the money the dances raised helped Gay McGill begin a new organization — Gay Montreal Association/Association Homophile de Montréal (GMA/AHM) — envisioned as "an umbrella organization" to finance and oversee all gay liberation activities in the city, English *and* French. The group began in January 1974, but by March, Front homosexuel québécois de libération (FHQL) was formed as an independent organization to counter the perceived inertia of the Anglophone dominated GMA/AHM. But FHQL disbanded by the end of 1974, and GMA/AHM would fold by early 1976, both due to organizational conflicts.

Organizing in Montreal was obviously quite challenging and erratic in the early days, but together these groups faced some forceful common enemies in the police and other official organizations. An early example occurred when a number of gay bars and clubs were forced to close after the Quebec liquor permit board refused to renew their licences in the lead up to Expo '67. This was part of an attempt to clean up the city's image in preparation for the event, and a significant rise in convictions for homosexual activities — 25 in 1960 versus 166 in 1964 — further suggested an organized effort.[23]

A similar but more extreme "crackdown" happened in the lead up to the 1976 Summer Olympics, when a campaign to "clean up" the city began. The Committee to Organize the Olympics later admitted a directive had been issued to drive "underground" the "non-conforming elements" of the city, including homosexuals.[24] Some examples of their work included a series of often-violent raids on bathhouses and clubs in 1975 and 1976, cumulatively resulting in the arrests of hundreds of men. It also resulted in a June 1976 protest that united the Montreal community against the "Olympic crackdown" in what was then the largest queer-related demonstration in Canadian history.

But the Montreal community's greatest challenge with the authorities was yet to come. As with previously noted examples in Edmonton and Toronto, Montreal had its own monumental police raid in October 1977, when fifty officers with bulletproof vests and machine guns raided the gay bar Truxx. The raid resulted in 146 men being charged as "found-ins at a common bawdy house," and the bar's owner charged as the "keeper of a common bawdy house."[25] Those charged were held in overcrowded cells, were unable to contact lawyers, and were forced to take venereal disease tests. Despite a mass community response where over 2000 people demonstrated in downtown Montreal, raids continued well into the 1980s, most notably at the bar Bud's in 1984 when 163 people were arrested. However, the Truxx rebellion helped create the preconditions necessary for the quiet introduction of sexual orientation protection in the province.

Also notable are the many assumptions about Quebec's progressive tendencies at the level of policy change and legal change. Quebec is an overwhelmingly secular society, then as now, and the church hierarchy exercises almost no political influence, but this did not result in a particularly less homophobic setting for the Quebec community in the first decade or two of organizing. As we will see in the next chapter, while Quebec was a pioneer in terms of a few key legislative matters, in many other cases the province was more or less on par with the rest of the country in terms of advancements for queer citizens.

Atlantic Canada

As one might expect, Halifax has been and continues to be the queer centre of Atlantic Canada. The Gay Alliance for Equality (GAE) was officially formed in Halifax on June 4, 1972. The group established a telephone counselling service (GAE Line) and operated a drop-in centre. Robin Metcalfe, one of the dominant organizers in GAE, explained that one of the unique elements of Halifax's organizing was that it owned its own social space, The Turret (London, Ontario, provides the only other example of this occurring). This raised substantial funds for community projects.[26]

Halifax's activist community was largely made up of working-class individuals in stark contrast to most other communities, where predominantly university students, academics and civil servants made up the groups. It was also distinctive in that it contained a relatively equal mix of men and women. Saskatoon and Ottawa were other communities where this was generally the case, though in all three cases this is not to suggest there were not conflicts between the genders.

The community was not particularly active politically, though in February 1977, GAE picketed CBC Radio when they refused to air a public service announcement for their phone line and counselling service. This was the first public queer-related demonstration in the history of Atlantic Canada. GAE also played a large role through the 1980s in fighting for protection from discrimination in Nova Scotia's human rights legislation.

Outside of Halifax, the first group in New Brunswick was formed by Keith Sly in Fredericton in February 1974. Called Gay Friends, the group only lasted until August 1975 and only ever had three active members. St. John's, Newfoundland, was much more successful with the Community Homophile Association of Newfoundland, which formed in 1974 and was active for six years.

Small Communities and Rural Areas

Throughout this chapter, every mention of an event or organization occurred in some of the country's largest urban areas. It is a simple fact that gay politics are usually pursued in urban areas, for all sorts of political and demographic reasons. This isn't to say that queer people don't live in rural regions and that those people don't have their own history.[27] It is important to understand that queer people living in smaller communities, and especially rural areas, are often faced with a different set of challenges than those in big cities. Living invisibly was a key to surviving even as lesbian and gay liberation thrived in urban areas. Bigotry and homophobic violence was and largely remains substantial in rural areas.

Organizing efforts from urban areas to reach out to rural queers did take place. For example, the Saskatchewan Gay Coalition was formed in 1977 by Saskatoon's Doug Wilson to offer outreach, networking and education. Wilson ended up building a mailing list of over 750 names, sending out a newsletter to help isolated queer people feel connected to larger communities and concerns.[28]

Smaller cities did eventually see their own queer organizing — mainly in the 1980s and 1990s — though groups were often difficult to maintain. These included Northern Lambda Nord, which formed in 1980 and served rural gays and lesbians in New Brunswick and Northern Maine by circulating a newsletter and trying to establish a sense of community. But it wasn't easy. As one of the founders, Jacques Lapointe, noted in a 1982 *Body Politic* interview, "You've got to be extremely courageous to be gay in rural areas."[29]

This was also true of queer people living in Northern Canada, where no official organizing occurred until the late 1980s when a small group of Yukon lesbians and gay men started having potlucks and barbeques. These would eventually lead to the formation of the Gay and Lesbian Alliance of the Yukon, which at one point had a mailing list of over 100 people from almost every Yukon community.[30] It wasn't until ten years later that the Northwest Territories followed suit with the formation of Out North, a group that organized Gay Pride events in Yellowknife in June 1997.

An optimal resource for learning more about the queer Canadian rural experience is Michael Riordan's *Out Our Way: Gay and Lesbian Life in the County*. Riordan, a rural queer by choice after leaving Toronto in the mid-1980s, writes, "When mainstream culture notices gay and lesbian folk, it tends to see us as urban. And our own media-makers have their hands full transmitting the stories of lesbian and gay downtowners. But more and more of us are choosing to live wherever it suits us. This is a free country, no?"[31] Riordan also noted something imperative to this discussion: "You'll find very few people of colour in this book, alas. By and large rural areas are about as welcoming to them as to homos, only we can hide better than they can."

Cross-Canada Organizing

All of this segregated discussion should not imply that cross-country organizing hasn't occurred, and it would be irresponsible to exclude mention of it. One of the first examples — and still one of the most powerful — came in 1971, when the first large-scale public gay demonstration was held in Canada. Over 200 people marched on Parliament Hill in the pouring rain for forty minutes, while another twenty marched in solidarity in Vancouver. Their primary purpose was to present "We Demand," a thirteen-page brief containing ten points calling for law reform and changes in public policy relating to homosexuals. Thirty years later, all but one demand — a uniform age of consent for all female and male homosexual and heterosexual acts — have been achieved.

Another key resource in cross-country organizing was the lesbian and gay liberation journal the *Body Politic*. While based in Toronto, people across the country interviewed for this book — who were present in queer organizing throughout the 1970s and 1980s — had no issue with calling the *Body Politic* a base of their political community during that time.

But beyond that, strong examples are somewhat rare. There was a series of national gay and lesbian rights coalitions in the 1970s and 1980s — most notably the National Gay Rights Coalition/Coalition nationale pour les droits des homosexuels, formed at the third national gay conference in 1975. Initially it consisted of twenty-seven different groups from across the country, and was renamed the Canadian Lesbian and Gay Rights Coalition in 1978. The group remained active until June 1980.

During federal elections, communities would rally together to ensure their issues were being heard. The first time was in 1972, when the National Gay Election Coalition brought together sixteen groups from across the country to intervene in the election that brought Pierre Trudeau to power for a second term.

Despite the existence of such organizations and events, there was simply not much interconnecting between communities. This was partially because — at least initially — most battles were fought against local and provincial institutions, and thus there was no real value in working as a national movement. When legal achievements did become more widespread, nationally organized groups did emerge in the 1980s. These new groups had a much different take on activism than most of those discussed in this chapter. While early groups wanted to politicize queer people and build communities, groups like the Canadian Association of Lesbians and Gay Men (CALGM) and Equality for Gays and Lesbians Everywhere (EGALE) saw equality rights as the main goal. Unlike previously mentioned national groups, which were coalitions of local grassroots organizations, these groups were made up of individual members.

As Miriam Smith notes in *Lesbian and Gay Rights in Canada*, EGALE in particular had members that were largely an emerging middle-class community of lesbians and gays who saw economic benefits in the legal recognition of same-sex relationships.[32] As we will see in the next chapter on legal reform, they represented a drastic change in how queer Canadians were organizing.

It is notable, however, that the advent of social media through the internet has presented new opportunities for community building and activism in recent years. Both Facebook and Twitter have played significant roles in bringing queer communities together online, whether regionally or nationally. "One thing that really characterizes activism today is the internet," says Alan Wong, a Montreal activist who coordinates Affirm-Action, an annual event for queer ethnic minorities, two-spirited people and their allies. "People are able to connect, they're able to send out a mass amount of information to a mass amount of people, and this facilitates things… I can't really compare this to the 1970s or 1980s, because I wasn't there, but I think the effect new media has had on queer activism needs to be taken into consideration."[33]

The Twitter hashtag "#canqueer" allows people across Canada to engage and debate in discussions affecting Canadian queer people.

In 2010, that discussion helped bring together protests in Toronto surrounding Toronto Pride's banning of the group Queers Against Israeli Apartheid (QuAIA) from marching in the Pride parade. And on May 17, 2011, queers and their supporters gathered across the country (and around the world) for the International Day Against Homophobia through the utilization of Facebook event groups. Born out of the 2006 International Conference on LGBT Community Human Rights in Montreal, the event is intended to spread awareness about issues affecting queers in their own countries and across the world. Events took place in Vancouver, Calgary, Toronto, Halifax and many areas in between.

This may not be the kind of activism the lesbian and gay liberation movement envisioned of their successors (though how could they?), but it has effectively breathed new life into the idea of a "Canadian queer community."

3. LEGAL REFORM

There is absolutely no doubt that the relationship between Canadian law and the queer community has seen drastic and far-reaching improvements since official organizing first began. Just over forty years ago, homosexuality was illegal and could result in jail time and being labelled "a dangerous sexual offender." Today, queer Canadians enjoy some of the most progressive legislation in the world.

This happened largely through three stages of law reform. The first, decriminalization, saw activists in the late 1960s fight to have laws inspired by a moral conservative strategy of sexual regulation that prohibited the simple act of two same-sex persons having consensual sex overturned. The second stage, equality, involved having human rights protection enacted to prevent discrimination on the grounds of sexual orientation, particularly in areas such as employment and housing. This long battle culminated in a series of huge legal victories in the 1980s and 1990s, the most substantial of which was the reading of "sexual orientation" into Section 15 of the *Canadian Charter of Rights of Freedoms*. From this, the cases flowed into the third stage, relationship recognition, which saw laws giving equal treatment to same-sex relationships.

There are a few very important things to note when considering Canada's relatively newfound status as an international queer rights leader. First, attributing these strides forward to lawmakers or judges is inappropriate. Particularly in the 1970s and 1980s, these battles were largely won because activists fought long and hard for them. Second and most importantly, the battle is not over. Same-sex marriage is not the final frontier of the queer rights movement. There remain the questions of whether same-sex marriage is a progressive idea in the first place and, if it is, of who exactly benefits from it. It wasn't even an issue for most of the pioneers of the Canadian movement while some issues they did very much believe in — like sexual censorship and the decriminalization of many consensual sex acts — remain unresolved. There are still several fires burning, and this book will explore them, but first let us turn to the many remarkable fires that were put out, and exactly how that occurred.

Decriminalization

Modelled after the British equivalent, The Consolidated Statutes of Canada was created in 1859, and included "buggery" (a British term for "sodomy") as an offence punishable by death. In 1892, it was reclassified as an "offence against morality," which more broadly targeted all male homosexual activity. Notably, the laws contained no reference to lesbians until the 1950s. In *Coming Out: Homosexual Politics in Britain from the Nineteenth Century to the Present*, Jeffrey Weeks explains that this omission reflected the belief that "lesbian sexuality was either non-existent or should not be encouraged by being mentioned."[1] Changes to the code took place in 1948, and then again in 1961. These changes would brand gay men first as "criminal sexual psychopaths" and then as "dangerous sexual offenders," both charges that carried indeterminate prison sentences.[2] This meant that only a celibate homosexual could be assured of not going to prison, potentially for life.

In the 1960s, political and social consensus began building around decriminalization though overall social attitudes towards homosexuals remained intensely negative. This, like early Canadian law, was partially influenced by the British. In 1957, the British government released the Wolfenden Report, which argued against criminalizing homosexual sex acts, unless they occurred in public or involved youth. The report led to the 1967 decriminalization of homosexual acts between consenting adults in Britain. Two years later, Canada followed suit with the help of its first gay community organizations. Vancouver's Association for Social Knowledge (ASK) suggested a Wolfenden Report-type *Criminal Code* reform in a paper to the Criminal Law Subsection of the British Columbia Division of the Canadian Bar Association.

The country's first gay groups — referred to as homophile organizations — very much relied on support from some liberal psychiatrists and politicians, the courts and even religious organizations. In October 1964, Professor William Nicholls, an Anglican priest who was head of religious studies at the University of British Columbia, stated that criminal law "should be changed to permit homosexual acts in private between consenting adults, and that the church should encourage stable unions between homosexuals."[3] These sorts of statements went a long way, largely because they were made by heterosexuals.

An important figure in this first phase of legal reform was Everett George Klippert, a mechanic in the Northwest Territories who was first investigated by police in connection with an arson committed in 1965. He had no connection to the fire, but during the investigation, Klippert voluntarily admitted to having consensual sex with other men. As a result, he was arrested and sentenced to three years in prison. When a court-ordered psychiatrist assessed Klippert as "incurably homosexual," he was sentenced to indefinite imprisonment as a "dangerous sexual offender."[4] His appeal to the Court of Appeal for the Northwest Territories was rejected.

On November 7, 1967, Klippert's case finally reached the Supreme Court of Canada, and in a highly controversial move, it was dismissed in a 3–2 decision. The next day, New Democratic Party leader Tommy Douglas raised Klippert's name in the House

"We Demand" was a brief presented to the federal government in August 1971. Written and researched by Toronto Gay Action, it was supported by gay organizations across Canada. On August 28, 1971, over 200 people rallied on Parliament Hill in support of the brief. The action was the first of its kind in Canada. Here were the demands:

1. The removal of the nebulous terms "gross indecency" and "indecent act" from the *Criminal Code* and their replacement by a specific listing of offences, and the equalization of penalties for all remaining homosexual and heterosexual acts; and defining "in private" in the *Criminal Code* to mean a "condition of privacy."

2. Removal of "gross indecency" and "buggery" as grounds for indictment as a "dangerous sexual offender" and for vagrancy.

3. A uniform age of consent for all female and male homosexual and heterosexual acts.

4. The *Immigration Act* be amended so as to omit all references to homosexuals and "homosexualism."

5. The right of equal employment and promotion at all government levels for homosexuals.

6. The *Divorce Act* be amended so as to omit sodomy and homosexual acts as grounds for divorce; moreover, in divorce cases homosexuality per se should not preclude the equal right of child custody.

7. The right of homosexuals to serve in the Armed Forces and, therefore, the removal of provisions for convicting service personnel of conduct and/or acts legal under the *Criminal Code*; further, the rescinding of policy statements reflecting on the homosexual.

8. To know if it is a policy of the Royal Canadian Mounted Police to identify homosexuals within any area of government service and then question them concerning their sexuality and the sexuality of others; and if this is the policy we demand its immediate cessation and the destruction of all records obtained.

9. All legal rights for homosexuals which currently exist for heterosexuals.
10. All public officials and law enforcement agents to employ the full force of their office to bring about changes in the negative attitudes and de facto expressions of discrimination and prejudice against homosexuals.

For the complete document, see "We Demand: The August 28th Gay Day Committee," *The Body Politic*, November/December 1971.

of Commons, stating that homosexuality should not be considered a criminal issue. For once, even the mainstream media, which had gone into a frenzy over the decision, largely agreed. Six weeks later, Pierre Trudeau (then justice minister of Canada, he would become prime minister the following April) introduced Bill C-150 into the House of Commons, and famously proclaimed, "the state has no place in the bedrooms of nation." One part of the bill would decriminalize homosexual acts between two consenting adults if they were twenty-one years of age or older. Representatives of the "homophile" community weren't entirely impressed. At the fourth annual North American Conference of Homophile Organizations (NACHO) in August 1968, they adopted a resolution harshly criticizing the age of consent limitations in Bill C-150.

When Bill C-150 was finally discussed in the House of Commons in the spring of 1969, Justice Minister John Turner declared that it was not intended to condone, endorse or encourage homosexuality and that it "doesn't even legalize this kind of conduct."[5] Instead, "it lifted the taint or stigma of the law" from these sexual acts. Despite numerous complaints from the more conservative political parties that the bill was "bringing the morals and values of skid row into the salons and drawing rooms of the nation," the bill passed by a vote of 149 to 55, and came into effect on August 26, 1969. Despite this, Klippert would remain in prison until July 21, 1971.[6]

While these events set the stage for the emergence of lesbian and gay liberation groups and their quest for equality, Bill C-150 itself was not as extensive a victory as it may appear. For one, the record of the debate of the bill in the House of Commons was described by George Smith as perhaps "the most heterosexist document in Canadian government history."[7] Moreover, it led to a limited form of decriminalization that did not actually legalize homosexuality itself and allowed for the continued regulation of queer sex. A Canadian coalition of gay and lesbian liberation groups was quick to point out this aspect in the 1971 public statement "We Demand":

> In 1969, the *Criminal Code* was amended so as to make certain sexual acts between consenting adults, in private, legal. This was widely misunderstood as "legalizing" homosexuality and thus putting homosexuals on an equal basis with other Canadians. In fact, this amendment was merely a recognition of the non-enforceable nature of the *Criminal Code* as it existed. Consequently, its effects have done little to alleviate the oppression of homosexual men and women in Canada. In our daily lives we are still confronted with discrimination, police harassment, exploitation and pressures to conform, which deny our sexuality.[8]

Equality

The early 1970s saw the momentous surge in lesbian and gay organizing that led to the eventual passing of human rights laws. As noted with reference to specific communities in the previous chapter, activist organizations working within the ideology of lesbian and gay liberation emerged all over the country between 1970 and 1975. Driven by a newly adopted militancy in stark contrast to the tactics of homophile organizing, these groups made a lasting mark on the history of queer Canadians. Their goals and battles were certainly not limited to achieving human rights legislation, but these groups would bring the human rights of queer people from non-existent to what they are today. Tactics included sending letters and briefs to legislatures and politicians, meeting with representatives of human rights commissions, and protesting a variety of events. Examples of each are endless.

The first public action that centred on gay rights reform occurred in June 1972, when twenty-five members of Toronto groups CHAT and TGA joined in protest in front of the Ontario Legislature about the omission of a sexual orientation clause from Bill 199, an amendment to the *Ontario Human Rights Code* then being considered by the Legislature. Later that year, Vancouver's GATE sent a letter to B.C. Minister of Labour William King asking for amendments to the *British Columbia Human Rights Act* to outlaw discrimination based on sexual orientation. King's response was that he "found it rather difficult to conceive of a situation where a homosexual would be discriminated against unless his tendencies were of public knowledge."[9]

Throughout the 1970s, essentially every gay group across the country began compiling briefs on cases where homosexuals had been discriminated against and submitting them to their respective provincial human rights commissions. The first sign of potential success came in 1973, when the Saskatchewan Human Rights Commission responded to Saskatoon activists' demands by recommending the expansion of anti-discrimination legislation and equal opportunity programs in the province, including the outlawing of discrimination based on sexual orientation. This was the first time that a human rights commission in Canada had called for the inclusion of sexual orientation in human rights legislation, though the call was not successful.

The first actual victories were municipal. On October 10, 1973, after significant lobbying from GATE, Toronto City Council became the first legislative body in Canada to prohibit discrimination based on sexual orientation. The resolution passed by a vote of 15–1. The *Body Politic* called it "our first win."[10] Ottawa would follow suit in April 1976, followed by Windsor in March 1977. But it would not be until late 1977 that any major change would happen on a provincial or federal level, and this particular change was an isolated and unexpected one. In December 1977, a "quiet late night session" of the Quebec National Assembly amended the *Quebec Charter of Human Rights* to include sexual orientation, making Quebec the first province — and first political jurisdiction larger than a city or county in the entire world — to provide legal protection for homosexuals. Tom Warner suggests in *Never Going Back* that the decision was in part the result of the angry community response to the Truxx bathhouse raids earlier that year, which "caused unwelcome publicity for a government wanting to project a progressive image."[11] Shortly after the raids, activists demanded that the Quebec Human Rights Commission recommend a sexual orientation amendment in their charter. They did, and the government passed it very quickly and very quietly within a matter of days.

Sadly, this precedent did not spill over into the remaining provinces, where activist groups had to continue the fight for human rights legislation. The battle in Ontario was particularly intense as activists fought against an extraordinarily homophobic Progressive Conservative government well into the 1980s. Even with the seemingly left-wing New Democratic Party in power — albeit a minority government struggling to maintain public support — Manitoba's government failed to include sexual orientation in an amendment in 1984, despite it being recommended by the Manitoba Human Rights Commission and over sixty organizations, including the Manitoba Teacher's Society.[12] Similar situations occurred across the country, and the next provincial amendment did not occur again until 1986 in Ontario.

Although most of the legal victories would eventually occur in the 1980s and 1990s, one of the biggest battles for equality was won outside the courtroom in the decade before. In 1979, activist Michael Lynch wrote the *Body Politic* article "The End of the Human Rights Decade," which proudly declared:

There is now a gay community that sees itself, and is seen by others, as a political "minority." Gay life has been brought to public consciousness; the facts of oppression, real and undeniable, have been made known. The strategy built to achieve human rights legislation may have failed in that one aim, but it has been wildly successful in fulfilling the other, subsidiary goals which may finally prove more valuable than a few changes in law.[13]

In the years following Lynch's declaration, inarguably the greatest legislative advancement in the history of queer Canada was slowly beginning to take shape. In 1982 the *Canadian Charter of Rights and Freedoms* came into effect under Pierre Trudeau's Liberal government. Section 15 of the *Charter*, enacted three years later, assured equality and non-discrimination. While Section 15 did not explicitly include sexual orientation as a "prohibited ground of discrimination," it was written in an open-ended matter, so that courts could potentially interpret additional grounds for discrimination. For the first time, there was a significant sense that queer people could actually obtain legal protection of their rights. While the lesbian and gay liberationists of the 1970s generally *expected* their court cases to fail, but pursued them anyway to raise public consciousness and mobilize community, suddenly the equation was fundamentally altered.

From 1985 onwards, courts began to apply the equality guarantees of the *Charter* to queer-related cases and profound changes began to take place in legal reform. It did not happen immediately, and at first queer activists were uncertain just how much the *Charter* would help their cause. But two cases in particular gave considerable clarity to that question: *Egan and Nesbit v. Canada* and *Vriend v. Alberta.*

The former case concerned the application of James Egan (the same man noted as "Canada's first gay activist") for spousal benefits for his partner Jack Nesbit under Old Age Security. The case went to the Supreme Court, where four out of five judges decided that no discrimination occurred in the denial of the pension benefit. However, the judges also decided at the same time that "sexual

TABLE 1 Amendments to Human Rights Legislation to Include Sexual Orientation, by Jurisdiction

Jurisdiction	Year
Quebec	1977
Ontario	1986
Yukon	1987
Manitoba	1987
Nova Scotia	1991
New Brunswick	1992
British Columbia	1992
Saskatchewan	1993
Canada	1995
Prince Edward Island.	1998
Alberta	1998
Nunavut	1999
NWT	2002

orientation" should indeed be read into Section 15 of the *Charter*.[14] Though it was a contradictory and unenthusiastic decision — pension benefits apparently were a reasonable limit of discrimination based on sexual orientation — it set a monumental precedent that would effectively prohibit discrimination by employers, landlords, service providers and governments.

The growing jurisprudence that the *Charter* brought forth also led to the amendment of the *Canadian Human Rights Act*, via Bill C-41 in June 1995, as well as provincial human rights laws. Some provinces were more cooperative than others, with Ontario the first province to pass such legislation (in 1986) since Quebec nearly a decade earlier, and Manitoba and the Yukon (despite the latter having no organized queer groups at the time) doing so a year later. For a timeline of

> ### Section 15 of the *Canadian Charter of Rights and Freedoms*
>
> 15. (1) Every individual is equal before and under the law and has the right to the equal protection and equal benefit of the law without discrimination and, in particular, without discrimination based on race, national or ethnic origin, colour, religion, sex, age or mental or physical disability.
> (2) Subsection (1) does not preclude any law, program or activity that has as its object the amelioration of conditions of disadvantaged individuals or groups including those that are disadvantaged because of race, national or ethnic origin, colour, religion, sex, age or mental or physical disability.

each provincial amendment, see Table 1, though Alberta's situation warrants some extended discussion.

The aforementioned court battle, *Vriend v. Alberta*, was the catalyst for Alberta's amendment, which saw the Supreme Court of Canada forcing the province to include "sexual orientation" in its human rights legislation. This came after three decades of the intensely conservative Alberta government repeatedly refusing to do so, despite the efforts of local queer activists. As late as 1989, an Alberta cabinet minister declared in a speech that he could not support such an amendment because it would allow "homosexuals to teach in schools."[15] Oddly enough, one of said homosexual teachers would force the Alberta government into compliance with the *Charter*. In 1991, Delwin Vriend was fired from his employment at King's College, a Christian school in Edmonton. When offered the job in 1987, he disclosed his sexual orientation and was told it would not be a problem. But when Vriend started being more public about his sexuality, the college fired him because "homosexual practice goes against the Bible."[16] Vriend filed a complaint with the Alberta Human Rights Commission, which was refused. This led him to file a lawsuit arguing that Alberta's *Individual Rights Protection Act* (IRPA) did not adhere to Canada's *Charter*. After years of legal setbacks that featured some exceptional homophobia on behalf of Alberta's judiciary, the case made its way to the Supreme Court of Canada. On April 2, 1998, the Court unanimously agreed that IRPA's omission of sexual orientation denied rights guaranteed by the *Charter*.

The decision resulted in homophobic hysteria by Albertan conservatives, with openly gay Edmonton city councillor Michael Phair even receiving death threats.[17] Premier Ralph Klein — who has been one of the great villains in the narrative of official Canadian homophobia — attempted to use a constitutional provision to circumvent the court's ruling. Clearly many Albertans agreed with him, as dozens of letters to both the *Calgary Herald* and the *Edmonton Journal* equating homosexuality to sin, bestiality and pedophilia showed.[18] But in the end, the amendment went through, completing human rights protection across all provinces.

Relationship Recognition

As lesbian and gay liberationists gained ground in terms of civil rights through the *Charter*, the movement became more identified with reform, and less with liberationist ideology. The cause was also being fought more and more in the courtrooms, and not on the streets where a sense of community could be negotiated. The politics of these legal cases became more defined by the individuals and their lawyers, whereas legal decisions before this usually occurred in the context of social struggles and organizing. Essentially, rights were no longer a means to an end, as the liberationists had sought, but an end in themselves. This came out of a more assimilationist agenda to bring queers into mainstream society. The great example of this is same-sex marriage, which was never really on the agenda of lesbian and gay liberation. In fact, most queer liberationists dreamed of the day that marriage would be abolished altogether. "We took a constructionist view of homosexuality," Gerald Hannon, a liberation activist and one of the founders of the *Body Politic* said, "and thought that all people should be free of repressive social institutions like marriage that bring with it traditional gender and sex roles.

The government should be out of the marriage business period. We shouldn't be trying to get in."[19]

But we did get in, and did so at an accelerated speed relative to other stages in queer law reform. As David Rayside notes, the Canadian story regarding queer rights began like that of the United States. But in the 1990s, it "picked up enough speed that we can refer to 'take-off.' We see this in a few other countries, mostly in Northern Europe, but nowhere as clearly as the Canadian case."[20] How did this "take-off" take place? Initially, there was some liberationist involvement in the fight for relationship recognition, though this was more dominant in the earlier stages of the campaign. The Coalition for Lesbian and Gay Rights Ontario (CLGRO) — one of the few surviving gay and lesbian liberation organizations in the country — had a huge role in fighting for relationship recognition through the province's rocky road to Bill 167 in the early 1990s (though their involvement divided members unsure if it adhered to the liberationist agenda).[21] Bill 167 would not have granted legal recognition to same-sex marriages, but would have amended "spouse" and "marital status" to include lesbians and gays in 56 provincial laws. The CLGRO had taken advantage of a rare and relatively progressive NDP provincial government in Ontario at the time, putting significant pressure on the party to address their concerns.

But when the bill was drawn up, even members of the NDP caucus shied away from supporting it, fearing backlash in the upcoming provincial election or perhaps just showing their true homophobic colours. One NDP backbencher declared he would not support Bill 167 because "every time you walk down the street people would say 'there goes that guy who supports the queer people.'"[22] Due to a lack of consensus among the NDP caucus, resounding and aggressive disapproval from the provincial Progressive Conservative party (which would overwhelmingly take power in the province the following spring), and, as Gary Kinsman argues, not enough mobilization on behalf of queer activists, the bill finally failed in June 1994.[23] The night after it was defeated, 8000 people took to the streets in protest (it was the first public protest surrounding the bill, which was a little too late), and it proved "an important setback for lesbian and gay organizing" in that it put similar provincial and federal legislative initiatives on the backburner.[24]

It would not be until the 1999 case *M v. H* that the Supreme Court of Canada would once again help push things forward. The case involved a lesbian couple that split up after years of living together, one of whom sought support payments that the other had refused. The landmark decision ruled that the definition of spouse as a "man and woman" under Ontario's *Family Law Act* was unconstitutional based on the *Charter*, and gave the Ontario government six months to bring their law into line. They did so via Bill 5, which created a new category, "same sex partner," through which said partners would receive the same legal rights and responsibilities as common law heterosexual couples. In doing so, the government — led by Progressive Conservative Premier Mike Harris — also made clear it was being forced to pass the bill, notable in the bill's ridiculous name: *An Act to Amend Certain Statutes as a Result of the Supreme Court Decision in M v. H*.[25]

In February 2000, the federal government responded to *M v. H* with Bill C-23, which guaranteed a host of rights and benefits for same-sex partners, including child-care tax benefits, pension benefits for widowed spouses, tax breaks on retirement savings plans, even conjugal prison visits. It passed by a vote of 174–72, though activists were not impressed either by the fact that it did not include overdue amendments in the *Immigration Act*, or that the bill had been altered to appease opposition by leaving the definition of marriage as "the union of a man and a woman to the exclusion of all others."

But it would not be long before that would change, even if many governments begrudgingly accepted the mixed advances allowed so far. The fact that there was a real possibility that same-sex marriage could be legalized mobilized people who hadn't been part of queer activism thus far. Predominantly white, middle- and upper-class gays and lesbians who saw an economic advantage in the legal recognition of same-sex relationships donated money to the queer movement like never before. Their voice was heard through groups like EGALE, which differed from liberationist groups in their main strategy of lobbying MPs and government. At the peak of the same-sex marriage debate, EGALE and its spinoff, Canadians for Equal Marriage, raised nearly $1 million to intervene in court challenges and lobby Parliament. This helped move things along very quickly. In 2002, the Law Commission of Canada, Parliament's advisors, told Canada's justice minister that same-sex marriage should indeed be legalized, and that Bill C-23 was discriminatory. Shortly thereafter, the Canadian Human Rights Commission suggested the same. One by one, courts of appeal in various provinces deemed the ban on same-sex marriage unconstitutional, effectively legalizing it: Ontario on June 10, 2003; British Columbia on July 8, 2003; and Quebec on March 19, 2004.

As one might expect, there was considerable opposition from conservative groups and politicians. In September 2003, future prime minister and then Canadian Alliance Leader Stephen Harper accused the federal government of "stacking Canada's courts with liberal-minded judges over the years in a covert effort to legislate same-sex marriage."[26] "They wanted to introduce this 'same-sex marriage' through back channels," Harper told reporters. "They didn't want to come to Parliament. They didn't want to go to the Canadian people and be honest that this is what they wanted. They had the courts do it for them, put the judges in they wanted, then they failed to appeal, failed to fight the case in the court."[27] Harper went so far as to introduce a motion in September 2003 that called on Parliament to preserve the definition of marriage as, once again, "the union of a man and a woman to the exclusion of all others."

But the motion narrowly failed by a vote of 137–132, a ratio that seemed to reflect the Canadian public. An SES Research poll in September 2003 showed that 47 percent of Canadians supported same-sex marriage, while 44 percent opposed it. Notably, support was highest in Quebec and British Columbia at 53 percent, and lowest in Alberta at just 28 percent.[28] This was a large increase from just six years earlier, when 63 percent of Canadians opposed it.

By the end of 2004, every province but New Brunswick, Prince Edward Island and Alberta had legalized gay marriage. At this point, Prime Minister Paul Martin announced in Parliament that Bill C-38 would be introduced to expand marriage rights to same-sex couples. Much debate and acrimony divided Parliament, with many Liberals and all Conservatives against the idea. But on June 28, 2005, the bill passed its final reading with a vote of 158–133. Less than a month later, it received royal assent, making Canada the fourth country in the world to legalize same-sex marriage (after the Netherlands, Belgium and Spain). Expectedly, Alberta — which had not legalized it independently at that time — tried to fight the decision, with Premier Ralph Klein even suggesting the Alberta government would stop solemnizing marriages altogether. But Alberta was forced to obey the legislation and — "much to our chagrin" as Klein publicly stated — the Alberta government began allowing same-sex marriages.[29]

There is no denying the monumental dramatics of this narrative, or that this kind of formal recognition is productive in a certain sense. Many queer Canadians clearly have embraced the decision (see Table 2), and despite the ideology of lesbian and gay liberationists, even they could understand why same-sex marriage had its importance. "Either you're equal or you're not," one said in an interview, "and when you are that means something."[30]

But there remains the justified liberationist notion that same-sex marriage should not be viewed as some sort of legal end game in the fight for queer rights. Even beyond the argument that marriage is an oppressive and state-sanctioned institution that should have never been a goal in the first place, there is the simpler question of whom exactly marriage serves. Like heterosexuals, not every queer person *wants* to get married, nor do they always end up in relationships that warrant marriages even if they wanted them to. It brings up the issue of the law's privileging of conjugal relationships. An imperative study written by Brenda Cossman for the Law Commission of Canada

TABLE 2 Statistics on Same-Sex Marriage through October 2006

Jurisdiction	Date of legalization	Number of same-sex marriages	Number of same-sex couples*
Ontario	June 10, 2003	3,765	17,510
British Columbia	July 8, 2003	1,370	7,035
Quebec	March 19, 2004	1,260	13,685
Yukon	July 14, 2004	10	30
Manitoba	September 16, 2004	100	935
Nova Scotia	September 24, 2004	140	1,255
Saskatchewan	November 5, 2004	100	565
Newfoundland and Labrador	December 21, 2004	50	310
New Brunswick	June 23, 2005	125	770
Alberta	July 20, 2005	510	3,055
Prince Edward Island	July 20, 2005	15	140
Northwest Territories	July 20, 2005	15	40
Nunavut	July 20, 2005	10	15
Canada	July 20, 2005	7,465	45,345

*Refers to same-sex couples that completed census
Source: Statistics Canada, Census of Population, 2006

argues that governments need to pursue a "more comprehensive and principled approach" to the legal recognition and support of the "full range of close personal relationships among adults," not just those who cohabitate under romantic circumstances.[31]

Essentially, same-sex marriage only serves people who are in a position to take advantage of such expanded recognition. It also maintains the idea of heterosexual marriage as a "norm" to which queer people should aspire. And as we will see, it leaves many other important issues out in the cold.

Sex and Censorship

While the remaining chapters in this book will take on some of the most outstanding examples of other issues facing today's queer people, notably education and health, a few issues remain that fall in the realm of law and public policy.

Sex and censorship comprise an enormous and complex set of issues in the Canadian queer narrative that warrant substantially more discussion. There are numerous works noted at the end of this book that provide much more extensive analysis. But for the purposes of understanding the legal issues that don't quite fit into the "three stages" of this chapter, we will briefly delve into them.[32]

Issues surrounding sex and censorship have always been contentious, even within the queer community. Though liberationists put them at the forefront of their movement, more conservative activists have been uneasy taking up many of these issues, especially where the sexuality of youth is involved. In 1972, the *Body Politic* published an article, "Of Men and Boys" by Gerald Hannon, that discussed the sexual relationship between older and younger men. When Toronto-area newspapers caused an uproar about the article, suggesting it "counseled the seduction of young boys," the local lesbian and gay organization CHAT publicly dissociated itself from the article.[33]

As one may imagine, mainstream Canadian society has been even more inhospitable to these sorts of issues. When a similarly themed article entitled "Men Loving Men Loving Boys," also written by Hannon, was published in the *Body Politic* five years later, the newspapers again took notice with very critical editorials. Except this time the furor in the papers led to a police raid on the *Body Politic* offices. The raid resulted in a six-year legal battle that saw two provincial court trials, three other separate court actions, six appeals, two trips to the Supreme Court of Canada and over $100,000 in legal fees. The charge against Hannon and fellow *Body Politic* writers Ed Jackson and Ken Popert were for "using the mails to transmit immoral or indecent material."[34]

It is important to note that the charges against the *Body Politic* came in the midst of a trial surrounding the rape and murder in Toronto of twelve-year-old shoeshine boy Emanuel Jacques by a group of men. The murder had brought forth a hysterically homophobic climate that classified gay men as predators of children, and the *Body Politic* article became a target. While in the end Hannon, Jackson, and Popert were acquitted, the emotional and financial costs of the ordeal were devastating. It also made clear that if there was one thing mainstream society was uncomfortable with regarding queer people, it was their relationship with children.

Many similar, though often less dramatic, acts of censorship have occurred, and much energy in the lesbian and gay liberation movement has been directed toward them and other issues surrounding sex. The abolition of age-of-consent laws, removal of pornography legislation, state-sanctioned obscenity determinations and "bawdyhouse" laws (used in both bathhouse and bar raids targeting homosexual people) are examples. The divisiveness surrounding these issues varied (the former two were far more controversial within the queer community than the latter two), but they were all issues that received a lot of attention. But when the mid-1980s brought forth a drastic shift in advocacy, new groups showed little interest in taking these issues on. Though there are countless examples of how more controversial topics were sidestepped by the focus on rights recognition and, more dominantly, same-sex marriage, the case of Little Sister's Book and Art Emporium is by far the most epic, and truly one of the most important legal battles regarding freedom of expression — queer or otherwise — in Canadian history.

A lesbian and gay bookstore in Vancouver, Little Sister's, like its Toronto counterpart Glad Day Bookshop, was a huge target of Canada Customs during an intensified period of harassment in the late 1980s and early 1990s (though this kind of censorship was present beforehand). Changes to censorship laws had been required following a 1985 Federal Court of Appeal decision that freedom of expression rights guaranteed by the *Charter* did not fall in line with provisions permitting the seizure of "immoral or indecent" materials. The response to this was Memorandum D-9-11, which had been introduced by the Conservative Mulroney government and changed very little. It still allowed for the seizure or banning of any material "containing depictions or descriptions of anal penetration, including depictions or descriptions involving implements of all kinds," and worse, gave Customs officials "the authority to use their own personal judgment as to what qualified as obscene."[35]

By 1990, nearly 75 percent of all books and magazines being shipped to queer-related bookstores were being seized.[36] At this point, Little Sister's was already in the midst of their battle with Canada Customs. By December 1996, Customs had seized more than 600 books and magazines from the store, and were not showing any signs of stopping. So the Vancouver community rallied to help the store hire a lawyer and fund the extraordinarily costly process — which several times nearly put the store out of business — of a *Charter* challenge against Canada Customs.

The trial was continuously delayed, did not begin until late 1994, and provided a book's worth of fascinating material (and a movie's worth, as exemplified by Aerlyn Weissman's must-see 2002 documentary *Little Sister's vs. Big Brother*). For example, testimony by a crown witness who had done a study of the effects on Customs officers of reviewing pornography found that 20 percent of the officers were themselves homophobic while over 70 percent "appeared to find homosexual acts repulsive."[37]

The trial ended with a mixed result in January 1996, when the B.C. Supreme Court ruled that Canada Customs had applied the law in a discriminatory manner against Little Sister's. However, they felt that the *administration* of the law was flawed, but not the law itself. Little Sister's appealed, and eventually met the Supreme Court of Canada in December 2000 where, once again, there was a disappointing decision. All nine judges believed Little Sister's had been targeted and harassed by Customs, but they did not find the existing definitions of obscenity threatening to freedom of expression.

Within a year of the Supreme Court ruling, Customs once again seized books from Little Sister's. They appealed again and another battle with Customs (now called the Canadian Border Services Agency) began. Except this time, Little Sister's couldn't raise the money necessary to go through with a trial, despite nearly $1 million being donated to the concurrent fight for same-sex marriage.[38] So where does that leave the issues? Largely unresolved. Even though Memorandum D-9-11 has been revised as recently as 2008, it still does suggest that most sexually explicit material involving adults is constitutionally protected expression. As recently as 2009, three gay-themed films were held at the border en route to Ottawa's lesbian and gay film festival.[39]

Beyond that issue, Section 197 of the Canadian *Criminal Code* still defines a "common bawdyhouse" as a public place "for the purposes of prostitution and the practices of acts of indecency." As we saw in the previous chapter, arrests made under the "common bawdyhouse" law in raids on bathhouses and bars have been a huge catalyst for queer activism over the years. They have occurred as recently as 1999 and 2000 (in Toronto), 2002 (in Calgary), 2003 (in Montreal) and 2004 (in Hamilton). That said, while Parliament has not shown any indication they will change the law, two 2005 companion cases — *R. v. Labaye* and *R. v. Kouri* — concerning two heterosexual "swingers" clubs in Montreal set a precedent. The decisions upheld consensual group sex and swinging activities in a club and alleged that "bawdyhouses" were consistent with personal autonomy and liberty.[40] However, the implications regarding queer sex have yet to be tested. The ruling does not preclude the bawdyhouse legislation being used against queer sex (although such convictions are likely to be much more difficult), and the use of liquor laws to police sexual behaviour in bathhouses remains a considerable threat.

Age-of-consent laws also remain problematic. Forty years ago, just after Bill C-150 half-heartedly decriminalized *some* forms of homosexual activity, we learned that early queer activists marched in Ottawa with ten demands. Nine of these have now been met, but one remains — "A uniform age of consent for all female and male homosexual and heterosexual acts." The age of consent in Canada is sixteen (raised from fourteen in 2008, much to the chagrin of many queer activists). However, the *Criminal Code of Canada* still states under section 159 that anal intercourse is illegal if either partner is under the age of *eighteen*, unless those partners are married. It is also still illegal to have anal sex when there are more than two parties involved (of any age), and if the anal intercourse takes place anywhere but in private, which is punishable with a $10,000 fine or six months in prison.[41] Though courts in Ontario (1995), Quebec (1998) and surprisingly, Alberta (2002) have independently declared Section 159 unconstitutional, the fact that it remains is a symbol of the official homophobia that lingers in Canada. It also potentially has an impact on youth sexuality and safer sex education and on the criminalization of young people for engaging in consensual sex. While same-sex marriage — in all its heteronormativity — may be legally available, same-sex *sex* is still clearly a point of discomfort. This is a major contradiction.

4. INSTITUTIONS

As noted in the introduction of this book, institutional homophobia can be seen as a response of heterosexism, which is the system that favours opposite-sex sexuality and relationships and presumes that everyone is heterosexual or that heterosexual attraction and relationships are the only norm, and therefore superior. This system is largely perpetrated by institutions, as Gary Kinsman notes in *The Regulation of Desire*:

> Until recently, heterosexuals rarely encountered visible gays, lesbians, or bisexuals. Most images were those projected by the mass media and those circulating in popular cultures, which generally came from psychology, sexology, the churches, and the courts and police. Dorothy E. Smith describes the 'ideological' circle through which the world is interpreted by the media and other agencies, this is one of the ways heterosexual hegemony operates. The world is interpreted through the schemas of 'expert sources' (police, policy analysts, government bureaucrats) and hegemonic cultural narratives to confirm the dominant interpretation of same-gender sexuality. 'Scientific' theories of homosexual deviance, criminality, or sickness thereby enter public discussion.[1]

Both the health and education sectors were noted at the end of the previous chapter as two institutions where queer people continue to face great obstacles and they will be the focus of the two chapters following this one. But heterosexism and institutional homophobia extends in almost every direction of Canadian society, as we have seen through examples pertaining to the judiciary, political parties, customs officials and many others.

Though the idea of homophobia and heterosexism within institutions is present in a wide variety of incarnations, this chapter will explore four areas in particular: the police, the RCMP and the military; employment and housing; religion and conservatism; and the media. Each offers a disturbing history of homophobia, and each has confirmed and — to varying degrees — still helps confirm the dominant interpretation of heterosexuality as the Canadian "norm" through their homophobic actions. In turn, they also offer some of the most inspiring examples in the queer rights movement.

The Police, the RCMP and the Military

The hostile relationship between the police and queer people has already been discussed in the first chapter of this book. Official homophobia and heterosexism on behalf of police and their organizations has been present longer than queer organizing. When the bill meant to decriminalize homosexuality was introduced in the late 1960s, the Canadian Association of Chiefs of Police opposed any changes to laws concerning homosexuality, their official reasoning being that it led to "depravity, blackmail, robbery and murder."[2] Chief Ken McIver of Calgary specifically said that passing the bill would represent "a decay in Canadian society" as homosexuality was "a horrible, vicious and terrible thing."[3] As we saw in the previous chapter, that bill did not end up fully decriminalizing queer sex and led to a criminal code that allowed the policing of queer sex outside of individuals' homes to continue with unfortunate ease.[4]

It was one thing for police officials to verbally denounce homosexuality to the public, it was quite another when they often exerted their power to violently disrupt the lives of queer people. Examples in Vancouver, Edmonton, Toronto and Montreal were just the tip of a horrifying iceberg. Throughout the 1970s and 1980s, and even into the 1990s and 2000s, police would often harass, entrap, arrest and even attack queer people.

Though this was predominantly directed at gay men in sex-oriented establishments like bathhouses, lesbians were not immune to police harassment. After being insulted and abused by a male patron, two women — Adrienne Potts and Pat Murphy — got up on stage and sang "I Enjoy Being a Dyke" (a play on the song "I Enjoy Being a Girl" from the musical *South Pacific*) at Toronto's Brunswick House Tavern in 1974. The tavern's management told them to leave, but after Potts, Murphy and their friends Sue Wells and Heather Beyer refused, police were called. Eight police officers dragged the women out of the bar, detained and harassed them. After being released, they returned to the bar to find witnesses but were again arrested. This spurred huge outrage in the Toronto community and the four women became known as The Brunswick Four.[5]

Though clearly the agenda of the police has been to morally regulate homosexuality, they actually played a significant role in mobilizing queer communities. The demonstrations resulting from major police raids remain some of the most iconic moments in the history of negotiating community within queer Canada. In was in large part because resistance to the 1981 raids in Toronto, for example, that Gay Liberation Against the Right Everywhere, Lesbians Against the Right and the Right to Privacy Committee joined forces to organize the first lesbian and gay Pride Day in the city.

Another extraordinary police-related narrative predates much of the context of this book. The Royal Canadian Mounted Police (RCMP), along with other enforcement groups, essentially spied on, interrogated and harassed gays and lesbians as "threats to society." Documented in Gary Kinsman and Patrizia Gentile's pivotal study *The Canadian War on Queers: National Security as Sexual Regulation*, this activity began in the midst of the Cold War–fuelled hysteria of the early 1950s. Essentially, homosexuals were seen as threats either because they were being associated with communism and potentially spying for the USSR, or because they were "easy targets for blackmail," and thus seen as a risk to national security.[6]

At first, the RCMP specifically targeted federal employees, spying on suspected homosexuals and then exposing them, and then often blackmailing them to expose others. But by the early 1960s, they expanded their surveillance to the general population. This led to a collection of more than 9000 names of suspected homosexuals in the Ottawa area by 1967. Most infamously, this process included "The Fruit Machine"; the RCMP put significant time, effort and money into attempting to invent a machine that would determine if a man was gay by recording changes in pupils dilation when shown erotic images of other men. The machine was partly funded by Health and Welfare Canada.

This kind of activity continued for quite some time. For example, demonstrations in Vancouver and Montreal were watched, and the 1971 launch of the *Body Politic* was considered so significant that the entire issue was included in RCMP files. *The Canadian War on Queers* explains that by the late 1970s and early 1980s, "the expansion of gay and lesbian community formation clashed with the sexual policing as raids and attacks replaced RCMP surveillance."[7]

Regarding employment, exclusionary practices in the RCMP and the armed forces officially ended in the 1980s and 1990s. In 1992 — at the same time the United States was enacting its "Don't Ask, Don't Tell" policy, allowing queers to serve in the military as long as they were not open about it, a policy that was not changed until 2010 — Justice Minister and Attorney General of Canada Kim Campbell announced that Canada was lifting its ban on homosexuals in the Canadian Forces, allowing them to serve openly and live on-base with their partners. This was in part thanks to Michelle Douglas, a lesbian who used the *Charter* to launch a constitutional challenge to her dismissal from the armed forces, which had been particularly suspicious of her "strong loyalty to members of the gay community."[8]

Relationships between queer communities and the local police forces, meanwhile, have also improved, beginning with the establishment of police liaison practices in the early and mid-1990s. However, this clearly did not entirely solve the problem. Police harassment continued throughout the decade and into the next, as the formation of police liaison committees was predicated on the assumption that the problem was one of communication, and not of the *Criminal Code* itself, which often directs cops against queer sex, or the heterosexist forms of police organizing that still very much exist.[9] However, meetings between police and queer representatives to discuss pertinent issues, sensitivity training for police officers, and in many cities, documenting anti-queer violence did help improve relations. By the end of the decade, there were many symbols of progress. In 1997, Vancouver's chief of police marched in the city's Pride parade with a small group of openly queer police officers. Just a few years earlier, it would have seemed impossible for a police officer to be "out" on the job.

But many in the community complained that not all police were taking the initiatives seriously enough, and there were clear examples of this. In 2000, Toronto police raided the Pussy Palace, an annual lesbian bathhouse event. The officers knocked down doors, took down names of women at the event and charged event organizers with three counts of "disorderly conduct" and one count each of "failing to provide sufficient security," "serving alcohol outside the prescribed area" and "serving liquor outside prescribed hours."[10] An Ontario Court stayed the charges and criticized the police for violating a constitutional right to privacy for the women at the Pussy Palace.

Raids of men's bathhouses occurred as late as 2004 in Hamilton and Calgary. Both those raids involved "bawdyhouse" charges, which the previous chapter noted should be difficult to administer after a precedent set in 2005. However, as was also noted, queer sex can still be constructed as acts of indecency, and police can also still utilize liquor laws to regulate homosexuality, as they did in the Pussy Palace incident. They can also simply administer heterosexist ideology in how they conduct their policing, as seen during the mass arrests at the G20 Summit in Toronto, where police brutality was a massive issue that mobilized protestors across the country. One of the allegations against the police was that they segregated the detained queer people from the rest of the detainees, telling them to "act" heterosexual for their own safety, despite the fact that the only presence of homophobia seemed to be from the police themselves.[11]

Employment and Housing

As with any other institution, individualized homophobia can be and still is present in interactions regarding employment and housing. That said, the *Charter* has at least officially granted full protection against discrimination based on sexual orientation in both regards. But there was a time when queer people were denied access to jobs or rental properties on a regular basis. Without the efforts of the women and men who fought against this discrimination, it would likely continue to be the case.

Early "victories" were appalling. In 1969, Paragraph 100 of the Report of the Royal Commission on Security recommended that homosexuals be allowed to work for the Public Service Commission, but that they "should not normally be granted clearance to higher levels, should not be recruited if there is a possibility that they may require such clearance in the course of their careers and should certainly not be posted to sensitive positions overseas."[12]

One of the most prominent queer civil rights cases in Canadian history came in 1975, when John Damien was asked to resign by the Ontario Racing Commission (an independent agency of the Ontario government) because he was gay. Damien — a true hero in Canadian queer history — had worked for Commission for five years, and at the time was one of the top three racing judges in Ontario. He refused to resign and was subsequently fired. In the decade that followed, Damien largely became the face of the struggle for human rights, and activists across the country became involved. In October 1977, coast-to-coast protests in Halifax, Montreal, Ottawa, Toronto, Windsor, Edmonton and Vancouver were held and organized as the National Gay Rights Coalition's Days of Protest for John Damien. This mobilization initially aided significantly in the crusade for human rights legislation. The publicity surrounding the case was huge and led to the first signs of political support in Ontario. But it came at a tremendous price. The defendants in the case — who had their legal fees paid by the government — used every trick in the book to the delay the case, causing serious emotional, physical and financial strife for Damien. He lost a serious amount of weight, went bankrupt and feared becoming homeless. In 1986 the defendants settled out of court, paying Damien only $50,000 — a year's salary plus interest — nowhere near what the legal battle had cost him. Tragically, Damien died of pancreatic cancer shortly after the settlement; just a few weeks after Ontario amended its human rights code to include sexual orientation.

Less severe examples of what Damien went through are literally countless and mostly undocumented. With regard to housing, one example indicative of hundreds of others occurred in December 1974, when five lesbians tried to rent a house in Waterloo, Ontario. The landlord agreed to rent it to them only if they paid extra money because "of the problems he believed were intrinsic to renting to homosexuals."[13] The women lodged a complaint with the Ontario Human Rights Commission (OHRC) but were told it had "no jurisdiction over this form of discrimination."

Human rights legislation via the *Charter* in the late 1980s and 1990s largely put a stop to these sorts of incidents, and helped substantially increase inclusiveness in the extension of employee benefits to same-sex partners (see Table 3 for a timeline for public employees). But it didn't fix things entirely. Having legislation against discrimination is one thing, but stopping discrimination in the first place is another. As recently as 2009, a landlord in the Northwest

TABLE 3 Extension of Federal, Provincial and Territorial Benefits for Same-Sex Partners of Public Employees of Canada

Year	Jurisdiction
1988	Yukon
1991	Ontario, Manitoba
1992	British Columbia, Northwest Territories
1993	New Brunswick, Quebec
1995	Nova Scotia
1997	Federal government
1998	Saskatchewan, Newfoundland
1999	Prince Edward Island, Nunavut
2002	Alberta

Source: David Rayside, *Queer Inclusions, Continental Divisions* (Toronto: University of Toronto Press, 2008), p. 98.

Territories refused to rent an apartment to a gay couple, saying "he feared God's wrath if he did." While the couple was successful in suing the landlord (though people less financially privileged might not have that option), the case also raised the issue of the landlord's freedom of religion and expression and how that too is protected by the *Canadian Charter of Rights and Freedoms*, and can be used as a loophole to anti-discrimination laws.[14]

The Religious Right

There are actually many progressive churches in Canada. During the campaign for same-sex marriage, legalization was supported by many Protestant, Jewish, Muslim, Buddhist and Quaker organizations. They provided large numbers of supporters and acted as a counter-argument to the conservative religious organizations that opposed same-sex marriage.

Historically, this kind of support is not uncommon. Even back in 1974, Rev. Bruce McLeod, moderator of the United Church of Canada, said in an interview, "Some of the great people in earth's history from Michelangelo on have been homosexuals. We would all be poorer without them."[15] On August 24, 1988, the United Church passed a resolution declaring that "all persons, regardless of sexual orientation, who profess their faith in Jesus Christ are welcome to be or become members of the United Church of Canada" and that "all members of the United Church are eligible to be considered for ordered ministry," making it the first major denomination in North America to support the ordination of gay and lesbian people.[16] This put the church at the forefront of a controversy that it has never shied away from, despite much opposition both from within its own membership and from other denominations. The United Church was also one of the first in Canada to begin performing gay marriages.

The Universal Fellowship of Metropolitan Community Churches, which has a specific outreach to queer people, came to Canada in 1973, opening official missions in both Toronto and Montreal. Its openly gay Toronto pastor Brent Hawkes proved an important figure in the Canadian queer community. Most famously, this was due to his gaining national attention by performing a same-sex wedding in January 2001, cleverly employing a loophole in Ontario law that allowed him to conduct a legal marriage without requiring prior government permission.[17] Though the government in turn refused to endorse the marriages, they were retroactively legalized when an Ontario court upheld them on June 10, 2003. Technically, this made them the first legal same-sex marriages in modern times.

However, these narratives do not compare in magnitude to the damage the "moral agenda" of more conservative religions — and conservatism in general — has done to queer people in adamantly reinforcing heterosexist norms.[18] As it is in the more publicized situation of the United States, Christian conservatism has provided one of the core oppositions to the queer movement, though as David Rayside explains, "the demographic and political weight is much less in Canada."[19] A 2004 poll noted that while 55 percent of

Americans agreed with the statement "religion is very important in my life," only 28 percent of Canadians said the same.[20] Despite being a relatively secular country (with regional variations; Quebec is the most secular and Alberta is the least), Canada has had its fair share of religion-fuelled heterosexism and institutionalized homophobia, much of it — just like lesbian and gay liberation itself — originating south of the border and migrating northwards.

When the lesbian and gay rights movement emerged in the 1970s, the conservative response in the United States was led by Rev. Jerry Falwell and Anita Bryant, an entertainer best known for appearing in television advertisements promoting Florida orange juice. Their Canadian allies included Rev. Ken Campbell of Renaissance Canada, who invited Bryant to bring her "Save the Children" campaign to Canada, which, among other things, fought to ban lesbian and gay teachers from schools. Her 1977 visit to Ontario prompted the largest gay and lesbian demonstration in Canada to that date, with 800 people marching up Yonge Street in Toronto. Campbell's crusade reached its height in the late 1970s and early 1980s, when he and Renaissance Canada aggressively targeted politicians who supported legislative initiatives to prohibit discrimination based on sexual orientation. They collaborated with social conservative politicians, with notable missions including defeating gay-friendly mayor John Sewell and openly gay city council candidate George Hislop in the 1980 Toronto municipal elections, and getting the Ontario provincial government to omit "sexual orientation" from its 1981 Human Rights Code amendments. They were successful on both fronts.

There's also a new generation of groups similar to the aggressively anti-gay U.S. Focus on the Family and the American Family Association often partly financed by such groups. Focus on the Family has a Canadian branch in British Columbia, and groups like Canada Family Action Coalition, the Evangelical Fellowship of Canada and REAL Women of Canada (which, in addition to be anti-gay, is also anti-feminist) have fought against queer rights. These groups also enthusiastically promote the idea that homosexuality is "curable." On its website, Focus on the Family has appealed to homosexuals who "seek to be cured": "You're not simply 'wired that way.' Indeed, you don't have to be gay — there is hope for those who want to change."[21]

These groups became vicious in the 2000s when same-sex marriage was at the forefront of the debate. And it wasn't simply Christian fundamentalists. When demonstrations against same-sex marriage hit Parliament Hill in 2005 — the biggest estimated at 15,000 participants — protesters included the Christian right, Sikhs, Jews and Muslims.[22] These conservative groups set aside their differences to lobby against same-sex marriage and even homosexuality in general.

Further examples of religiously sanctioned heterosexism are rampant throughout the history presented in this book, and religion has more of a stronghold on Canadian society than people might perceive. Almost every battle won has been won against the opposition of religious conservatism, and most of the battles that remain have been either indirectly or, in most cases, directly threatened by it. Even the *Charter of Rights and Freedoms* — the apparent golden ticket to queer human rights — proves problematic when it comes to religion. Like sexual orientation, religion is protected in the *Charter* under "freedom of religion and expression." This has allowed discrimination to be expressed freely under the guise of religious beliefs. This is certainly clear with respect to religious education systems, discussed in Chapter 6.

Also troubling are recent developments in the relationship between religious conservatism and Canadian politics, which have disturbed perceived notions of the separation of church and state. Conservative Party leader and current Prime Minister Stephen Harper perhaps sums up the situation best himself with this 2006 statement:

> In recent years, some politicians and commentators have asserted that in order to maintain separation of church

and state, legislators should not be influenced by religious belief… The notion of separation refers to the state not interfering in religious practice and treating all faith communities impartially. It does not mean that faith has no place in public life of the public square.[23]

It should be noted before discussing religion and conservatism any further that religion and social justice is another pairing that also has a major impact on Canadian politics. In particular, the CCF/NDP has always had members, most notably its leaders J. S. Woodsworth and Tommy Douglas, who were church ministers before they entered politics. However, Harper's Conservative Party attracts a disproportionate number of conservative Christians, and a 2006 poll showed that, of those who voted Conservative, 40 percent of Protestants attending church at least weekly pointed to moral issues like abortion and same-sex marriage as the area that mattered most in deciding which candidate to vote for.[24] It has been noted that there are strong links between Stephen Harper's inner circle and Christian right organizations, and that "subtle cues in [Harper's] public language signal to religiously traditional voters that he is one of them."[25]

Harper's government has definitely struggled in pushing forth their conservative agenda. Shortly after taking office in 2006, they brought forth a motion calling on the government to restore the traditional definition of marriage, which was defeated 175 to 123. That same year, a leak exposed that the Conservatives had been planning a "defence of religion act," which did not end up moving forward. This four-part legislation would have been aimed at protecting religious groups and believers from prosecution for human rights violations against gays and lesbians. For example, one aspect of the law would have protected people who speak out against queer people.[26]

These failed attempts at pushing this agenda speak to the fact that conservatism remains a minority belief system in Canada, much more so than in the United States. But while David Rayside argues that the Conservatives have "not been able to deliver observable change in policy on core concerns of its religious voters" and are unlikely to provide them with the capacity to "dominate religious right voting in the way the Republicans have [in America]," there are definitely causes for concern.[27] This is particularly true in the wake of Harper's 2011 majority government win, which gives the Conservatives considerably more power.

Even under a minority government, Harper appointed socially conservative judges to a court system that has proved pivotal in the legal reforms that have benefited the queer community. The Harper government also raised the age of consent from fourteen to sixteen, a decision condemned by every major queer lobby group because it created extra barriers to sexual health information for young people and raises the possibility of young queer people being arrested for consensual sex. They also abolished the Court Challenges Program, which significantly aided the queer community in funding *Charter* challenges. Without it, access to human rights protection is a privilege not all of us can afford.

The Media

The mainstream media have occasionally been friends of the queer community, and has at times been useful in providing an avenue to communicate to a society beyond them. That's much truer in the past decade or so than in earlier years of organizing, but there were examples then as well. For one, a 1964 *Macleans* article entitled "The Homosexual Next Door: A Sober Appraisal of a New Social Phenomenon," was the first full-scale article in a mainstream Canadian publication to take a generally, though not extensively, positive view of homosexuality. Written by Sidney Katz, the article was largely constructed through interviews with James Egan, Canada's first prominent gay activist. The Canadian Broadcasting Corporation (CBC) also brought early gay and lesbian activists to news programs to discuss their work. For example, in January 1970 the University of Toronto Homophile Association's Charles Hill, Graham Jackson and Ian Young appeared on Robert Fulford's CBC radio program to discuss lesbian and gay liberation. But, as these sorts of narratives tend to exemplify, problems occurred far more often than the relatively progressive examples. The mainstream media, particularly newspapers and magazines, have censored queer groups, been a platform for anti-gay organizations and have facilitated both heterosexist norms and homophobic hysteria through their editorial policies.

Throughout the early 1970s, the *Toronto Star* became infamous for refusing to publish gay- or lesbian-related advertisements. In 1973, they rejected a classified ad soliciting subscriptions for lesbian and gay liberation magazine the *Body Politic*. The ad simply read, "*The Body Politic*, Gay Liberation Journal, $2 for six issues. 4 Kensington Ave., Toronto, Ont. M5T 2J7."[28] The newspaper's response to the *Body Politic*'s subsequent complaint was that it was not their policy to "accept advertising which would identify or tend to identify a person as a homosexual or to carry advertisements relating to homosexual activity."[29] This was very common throughout Canada at the time. Other culprits included the *Vancouver Sun*, which on countless occasions refused to run ads with words like "gay" or "homosexual" in them. In 1974, their refusal to run a basic advertisement for Vancouver publication *Gay Tide* was noted with respect to that city's queer community and resulted in a lawsuit that went to the Supreme Court of Canada.

The mass media have also been responsible for sensationalizing gay scandals in ways that have caused serious harm to queer people. In 1975, sixteen clients of a "Male Modelling Agency" were arrested and charged in connection with a so-called "prostitution ring" in Ottawa. Both the *Ottawa Citizen* and the *Ottawa Journal* dubbed the event the "homosexual vice ring" scandal and consistently used the term "boys" in headlines to describe the young men involved in the charges being laid.[30] The phrase "vice ring" suggests that the men charged were involved in the organization of a prostitution service (they were not), and these "boys" were all between the ages of sixteen and twenty-one. Moreover, the newspapers — with the cooperation of the equally guilty police — listed the names of all those arrested, resulting in nine of the men losing their jobs, and one of them committing suicide.

The previously noted murder of Emanuel Jaques presents another example. When three men sexually assaulted and murdered twelve-year-old Jaques, Toronto newspapers went on a rampage against all queer men, portraying the murder as a "homosexual" one. Though clearly the murder was a horrific act of violence, as Gary Kinsman notes, "by constantly referring to [it as] a 'homosexual' murder, the media suggested a relationship between homosexual behaviour, pedophilia and murderous acts that cemented in the public mind."[31] Though these sorts of media incidents have grown less severe since the 1970s and 1980s, they have definitely not gone away. The *Toronto Sun* and now defunct right-wing magazine *Alberta Report* are two outstanding examples.

Alberta Report, one of the province's most prominent publications — during the 1990s it was actually one of the most widely read newsmagazines nationwide — had ties to conservative political and social organizations and ran some of the most anti-queer articles the Canadian mainstream media have ever produced. A 1996 article was entitled "An AIDS cure could increase gay promiscuity," while a year later they blended anti-queer sentiment with an anti-choice agenda when they asked on a cover, "Why do Canada's courts invent charter rights for gays and not for babies?"[32]

Alberta Report folded in 2003, but its ideology lives on. The *Toronto Sun* continues to produce heterosexism and homophobia through its editorials. Its record in doing so extends way back, from playing a substantial role in mobilizing police into raiding the *Body Politic* offices, to facilitating the anti-queer attacks during Toronto's 1980 election, to cooperating with police during the 1981 bathhouse raids. During the raids, the *Sun* published the names and addresses of those arrested, and founding editor Peter Worthington (who continues

Queer Artists

Queer media is certainly not limited to newspapers and magazines. Film, literature, music, theatre and visual art has played a remarkable role in the history of queer Canada, and continues to do so. Simply listing the queer Canadian photographers, painters, artist collectives, video artists, filmmakers, playwrights, poets, novelists, musicians and artistic institutions could take a whole chapter of this book and wouldn't even come close to doing them justice. But reading about how important these contributions are pales in comparison to experiencing them for yourself. The most constructive approach then is to offer two lists of suggestions for your own private introductory course: fifteen literary works, and fifteen films. Clearly this is reductive and excludes visual art, music and other forms,, but hopefully it's only the beginning of your relationship with the vast and imperative world of Canadian queer art.

to edit the paper as of 2011) told the CBC that "a person's sexual orientation or preferences should remain in the closet."[33]

Since then, Worthington has made numerous contributions to this anti-gay agenda. He wrote a 1994 opinion piece entitled "The Squalor of Gay Life," in 2000 called anti-gay talk show host Laura Schlessinger "a voice of morality" and in 2005 chimed in about same-sex marriage: "a homosexual has no role in perpetuating the species." In 2010 Worthington asked on the front page if openly gay Toronto mayoral candidate George Smitherman was "too gay."[34]

On the flipside, though, is the queer community's *own* media, which have worked actively against the ideology presented in the mainstream media and have often been a target in itself, as explained earlier in this chapter. But they also played a massive role in organizing community, both socially and politically. One of the earliest examples was Toronto-based magazine *Gay*, which began publishing in 1964. It contained articles on homosexuality, fiction, reviews and photos. It ceased publication by 1966, but made a lasting impression.[35] A decade later, Vancouver's aforementioned *Gay Tide* also proved hugely influential. It began publishing in August

15 Essential Canadian Queer Literary Works

The Desert of the Heart, Jane Rule (novel, 1964)
Place d'Armes, Scott Symons (novel, 1967)
The Male Muse: A Gay Anthology, Ian Young (poetry, 1973)
Hosanna, Michel Tremblay (play, 1974)
Nights in the Underground: An Exploration of Love, Marie-Claire Blais (novel, 1979)
Les feluettes, Michel Marc Bouchard (play, 1987)
Furious, Erin Mouré (poetry, 1988)
These Waves of Dying Friends, Michael Lynch (poetry, 1989)
Mauve Desert, Nicole Brossard (novel, 1990)
No Language Is Neutral, Dionne Brand (poetry, 1990)
Fall on Your Knees, Anne-Marie MacDonald (novel, 1996)
Kiss of the Fur Queen, Tomson Highway (novel, 1998)
Autobiography of Red: A Novel in Verse, Anne Carson (poetry, 1998)
I Still Love You, Daniel MacIvor (collection of plays, 2006)
Perfectly Abnormal: Seven Gay Plays, Sky Gilbert (collection of plays, 2006)

For an extensive discussion of Canadian queer literary works and an exhaustive list of suggested reads, see the catalogue for Scott Rayter, Donald McLeod and Maureen FitzGerald's exhibition "Queer CanLit: Canadian Lesbian, Gay, Bisexual and Transgender (LGBT) Literature in English," Thomas Fisher Rare Book Library, University of Toronto, 2008. Available for download at <https://tspace.library.utoronto.ca/bitstream/1807/16670/.../QueerCanLit06.pdf>.

1973 through the work of liberation group GATE, and continued to do so until March 1980.

Women-specific magazines were also an important part of the early days of the movement. Often in collaboration with feminist writers, they included Toronto's *Other Woman*, first published in 1972. Produced in cooperation with feminist newspapers *Bellyful* and *Velvet First*, the paper contained material written from a lesbian-feminist perspective and continued publishing through 1977. Montreal's *Long Time Coming*, produced by Montreal Gay Women, had a similar editorial policy and was published from 1973 to 1976. Though not entirely women-specific, in 1984 national magazine *Rites* began publishing and lasted nearly a decade. It "strove to give expression

15 Essential Canadian Queer Films

A tout prendre, Claude Jutra (1963)
Winter Kept Us Warm, David Secter (1965)
Montreal Main, Frank Vitale (1974)
Il était une fois dans l'Est, Andre Brassard and Michel Tremblay (1974)
Outrageous! Richard Brenner (1977)
Track Two, Harry Sutherland (1982)
Anne Trister, Lea Pool (1986)
Salut Victor! Anne Claire Poirier (1988)
No Skin off My Ass, Bruce LaBruce (1991)
Forbidden Love: The Unashamed Stories of Lesbian Lives, Lynn Fernie and Aerlyn Weissman (1992)
Zero Patience, John Greyson (1992)
When Night Is Falling, Patricia Rozema (1987)
Fire, Deepa Mehta (1996)
The Hanging Garden, Thom Fitzgerald (1997)
J'ai tue ma mère, Xavier Dolan (2009)

For a remarkable account and celebration of Canadian queer film, including a comprehensive encyclopedia of films, filmmakers, video artists and institutions, see Thomas Waugh, *The Romance of Transgression in Canada: Queering Sexualities, Nations, Cinemas* (Montreal: McGill-Queen's University Press, 2006).

to the connections between lesbian and gay oppression and the oppression of all women and the experience of other oppressions such as class, race and age."[36]

But the *Body Politic* — already mentioned numerous times — is clearly the iconic example of Canadian queer media. As described by Michael Riordan in the fifth anniversary issue of the magazine, the *Body Politic* was "born in the wild heat and ferment of Canada's first gay upheavals."[37] Launched October 28, 1971, when 5000 copies of its first issue went on sale across the country, it was the first real voice for queers in Canada. Because of the publication, "there was de facto communication [between all the communities] because in the 1970s and 1980s we all obtained bundles of the *Body Politic* from Toronto and we all read it cover to cover," Chris Vogel of Winnipeg said.[38] The *Body Politic* played a role in essentially every single battle fought in the lesbian and gay liberation movement (though notably was criticized for not recognizing marginal groups within the queer community). It was the first Canadian publication to write about AIDS, for example, in an issue with the article "'Gay' Cancer and Burning Flesh: The Media Didn't Investigate." An informal collective with no paid staff, it unfortunately folded in 1987, in part due to financial troubles.[39] Its publisher, Pink Triangle Press, more or less replaced it with the much more commercial and somewhat less politically minded *Xtra!*, which continues to this day.

Xtra!, along with its Vancouver and Ottawa spinoffs *Xtra! West* and *Xtra! Capitol*, have definitely helped fill the void, as have other current publications like Calgary-based *Outlooks*, Saskatoon-based *Perceptions* and Toronto-based *In Toronto*. But it's unlikely that any magazine will prove as relevant to the queer movement as the *Body Politic* was, at least not a print magazine. As noted at the end of Chapter 2, online social media have been slowly replacing print media as a mobilizing force.

5. CHILDREN, YOUTH AND EDUCATION

"Society loses much of its rationality when it comes to homosexuality and children," Bruce MacDougall wrote in a 1998 article for the *Saskatchewan Law Review*.[1] His strong words represent a myriad of issues that present perhaps the greatest barrier to rights for queer people. Whether in respect to educating them, parenting them or sexualizing them, much of Canadian society has proved quite hysterical when it comes to queer people or queer issues and their relationship to children and youth.

These sorts of attitudes are extremely problematic and often downright dangerous, in one sense, because of the considerable minority of young Canadians who are queer themselves. Historically, queer youth have been excluded from the adult queer community, in part because of age laws (both age-of-consent and liquor laws restricting access to bars) and because of apprehension on the part of adult queers to associate themselves with youth because of hostility from heterosexual society. But while the adult community has begun reaching out to their younger counterparts through the facilitation of queer-run youth groups and even a queer-oriented public school, major problems remain. Suicide is still the leading cause of death among queer youth, who account for about 30 percent of all successful suicide attempts.[2]

These statistics reveal a full-fledged epidemic, one that has gained quite a bit of attention during the 2000s. Progress has been made, with many school boards across the country being receptive to advocacy surrounding queer youth issues, such as drafting queer-positive curriculum, enacting policies on homophobia or encouraging gay-straight alliance clubs. But many school boards have entirely resisted such ideas, particularly within private, religion-oriented boards that aren't subject to the same regulations as public boards. These school boards have also been one of the final frontiers in employment discrimination when it comes to queer teachers. And schools remain a remarkably heterosexist form of socialization. Combating homophobia in schools is one thing, but making them places in which heterosexuality is not taught as the norm is another.[3]

In one sense, all of these attitudes are problematic because educating children and youth is a major key in combating homophobia and heterosexism. People are not born with these ideologies, they are taught them. They remain huge problems not only in Canada's education system, but also in the fabric of society, which perpetuates teaching new generations hateful belief systems. While young people today are generally less prejudiced toward queer people than any generation before them, homophobia and heterosexism remain indoctrinated into the socialization of Canada's children and youth.

Queer Parenting

Of all the issues expressed in this chapter, queer parenting has seen the most progress. As of 2011, Canada is widely considered one of the most liberal countries in the world in recognizing parenting relationships involving queer parents and their children. In the United States, recent elections saw propositions pass favouring a constitutional ban prohibiting lesbians and gays from adopting children. In Canada, all provinces and territories support adoption by queer parents except the Yukon and Nunavut (where the laws are ambiguous though likely to support it as well).

Historically, as one might expect, this was far from the case.

When British Columbia extended adoption rights to same-sex couples in 1995, which made it the first jurisdiction in the world to do so, the nationwide view on the topic was highly divided. For example, when Bill 167 was defeated in Ontario in 1994, many said it was because of anxiety over the inclusion of adoption rights. "Acknowledging rights and responsibilities for same-sex couples was one thing, and still controversial for sure," David Rayside noted of the climate in the mid-1990s. "But bringing children into the picture engendered much more fear."[4]

The first recorded case to focus on the custody of a child to a queer parent came in 1974, when Darlene Case of Saskatoon lost custody of her two children to her ex-husband. She had been granted custody in 1973 but the decision was reversed after the ex-husband appealed based on Case's lesbianism. At this time, there was no precedent in Canada for an openly lesbian or gay man gaining or retaining child custody. "It seems to me that homosexuality on the part of a parent is a factor to be considered along with all of the other evidence in the case," the judge had said at the time.[5]

An important contributor to the fight for custody rights during this time was the Lesbian Mothers Defence Fund, founded in Toronto in 1979 to offer financial and moral support for women. In 1983 they were noted as having helped "almost two dozen women keep or win custody, usually through out of court settlements."[6]

By the mid-1980s, there were frequent examples of favourable judicial decisions with regard to queer parents, though often the cases still would see homophobic judicial attitudes alongside them. In 1986, the case *Templeman v. Templeman* saw a divorced mother and father battle over two children. The marriage had dissolved after the father had realized he was gay. While the court ended up giving custody to the father, it noted, despite absolutely no factual basis for such a concern: "In the event that the respondent [father] exposes his children to a promiscuous lifestyle or to harmful influences, the petitioner of course, has the right to vary these access provisions."[7] The judicial homophobia present in this case brings up the arguments suggesting that lesbians have faced less resistance than gay men with regard to adoption. Darryl Wishard claims "more courts have granted lesbian mothers the right to custody of their children than have granted custody to homosexual fathers."[8] Explanations for this include a general preference for maternal custody, assumptions regarding gay men and either pedophilia or recklessly promiscuous "lifestyles" (as we saw with *Templeman*) and AIDS phobias. But Katherine Arnup, a leading writer on lesbian parenting battles, suggests the claim cannot be upheld "without much more quantitative evidence." She argues that the discrepancy may be because gay men choose not to seek custody, "either because they are afraid that their custodial bid will be unsuccessful, or, perhaps more commonly, because they, like their heterosexual counterparts, do not wish to have primary care and custody of their children."[9]

With respect to all queer parents, however, things did begin improving substantially in the mid-1990s. For the first time, courts were recognizing the parental status of non-biological parents, and chapters of the Children's Aid Society were declaring that they would welcome queer foster parents. By 1999, British Columbia, Ontario, Saskatchewan and, surprisingly, Alberta, had legalized forms of same-sex adoption. By 2004 formal recognition of queer parents was extensive across the country (see Table 4).

The narrative surrounding rights for queer parenting occurred within a similar timeframe as relationship recognition. But unlike relationship recognition, which met a much more concrete end result in same-sex marriage, queer parenting presents a more complex set of laws and goals to be achieved for inequalities to be abolished. Heterosexism can be and often still is present in adoption agencies, foster placement, family courts and fertility clinics. One study in the 1990s said that 84 percent of adoption workers "would reject an application from a woman in a stable lesbian relationship."[10] Things have surely progressed since then, but as recently as 2005, a Strategic Council poll showed that only 48 percent of Canadians were supportive of queer parents.[11] That's a sizeable number compared to

TABLE 4 Canadian Provincial Recognition of Adoption Rights of Same-Sex Couples, 1995–2004

Year	Province	Type	Process
1995	Ontario	step-parent and joint*	court
1995	British Columbia	step-parent and joint**	legislation
1998	Saskatchewan	joint adoption***	legislation
1999	Alberta	step-parent	court & legislation
2001	Nova Scotia	step-parent and joint	court & legislation
2002	Saskatchewan	step-parent	legislation
2002	Newfoundland	step-parent and joint	legislation
2002	Manitoba	step-parent and joint	legislation
2002	Quebec	full rights****	legislation
2002	Northwest Territories	step-parent and joint	legislation
2004	New Brunswick	step-parent	human rights tribunal

* Later (1999) read as including joint adoption.
** The B.C. adoption law was passed in 1995 but came into effect in 1996.
*** Partial change in 1998, redefinition of spouse in 2001.
**** The civil union legislation of 2002 allowed women who had engaged in a "parental plan" to both be registered on the child's birth certificate.
Source: David Rayside, *Queer Inclusions, Continental Divisions* (Toronto: University of Toronto Press, 2008), p. 179.

say, 1988, when only 25 percent thought so,[12] but it still suggests that just over half the country is averse to the idea, and some of that half hold power in the process of queer people becoming parents.

And the issues run deeper than that. On the formal side of things, queer Canadians trying to adopt overseas are faced with much greater obstacles than their heterosexual counterparts. China, for example, requires applicants to declare formally that they are not lesbian or gay. And then there are obstacles that result from general societal attitudes and structures. Queer parents and their children are likely to deal with considerable prejudice in the education system, the health industry and a variety of other institutions. And opportunities for queer parents vary drastically by class. Both adoption and reproductive assistance can prove quite expensive, not to mention the classism in the adoption and foster parent system that views wealth as a determinant of a "worthy home."

Queer Teachers

Moral panic over the issue of queer people teaching in education facilities has featured prominently in the history of institutional homophobia, as we have seen regarding the firing of Delwin Vriend. Socially conservative organizations and homophobic parents or school officials alike have long sought to exclude queer people from teaching children or youth simply because they are queer. Ideologies that associate queers with pedophilia or suggest that queers have the ability to "recruit" children into becoming queer themselves have been relayed repeatedly in this heterosexist quest, and many teachers have had their professional lives destroyed as a result.

Besides Vriend, another example of this occurred in 1976 with the case of Doug Wilson. A graduate student at the College of Education at the University of Saskatchewan, Wilson was employed as a sessional lecturer. When the dean of education learned that Wilson — active in the lesbian and gay liberation community in Saskatoon — had advertised for people interested in joining an "academic gay association" in the student newspaper, he was told he would no longer be allowed to supervise students. Wilson filed a complaint with the Human Rights Commission and the university was sent a notice of formal inquiry, alleging that it had discriminated "in regard to his employment or any term of his employment by refusing to allow him to supervise practice teachers because of his sex, and in particular because he is a homosexual, contrary to Section 3 of the *Fair Employment Practices Act*."[13] The *Fair Employment Practices Act* forbade discrimination based on "sex." In the end, the court held that Wilson had been discriminated against based on his sexual orientation, not his sex, which they agreed did not include sexual orientation. Though ultimately unsuccessful, Wilson's battle was important in raising awareness nationally as it was covered nationwide in both the mainstream and queer press. It is discussed at length in David Geiss's 2009 documentary *Stubblejumper*.

Like most discrimination involving employment practices, it became much more difficult for queers to be treated in the manner Wilson was once the *Charter* was applied in similar discrimination cases. But many queer teachers are still subject to a homophobic work environment. In 2000, a situation involving a Grade 4 teacher at an elementary public school in Ontario's Peel District School Board exemplified this. The teacher — a lesbian — brought a female companion to a school social event. When her students asked her who the woman was, she told them that she was her lesbian partner. Some parents were outraged, and the school's principal sent a letter home with students that said "the manner in which the discussion unfolded was not consistent with the board protocol."[14] Worse, a spokesperson for the school board described the teacher's action as "an error in judgment," and a trustee officially said that "there was no educational value" in what she did.[15] David Rayside notes that "this story could easily be repeated in school boards across Canada, many of which impose strict guidelines on discussion of sensitive issues, with 'human sexuality' regularly cited as an example."[16]

But beyond having to exert caution in being "too out" on the job, queer teachers' jobs in themselves are still at risk. In April 2010, Lisa Reimer, a lesbian who taught at Little Flower Academy, a Catholic school in Vancouver, alleged that she was fired because she and her partner had become parents. Reimer was told the parents of students at the school were worried "the girls might follow Ms. Reimer's lead."[17] The school denied the allegations, and Reimer has yet to pursue legal action officially, but the incident speaks to a very real concern.

Beyond the fact that there is little government control over what they can teach (at least in the vast majority of the country), religious schools have a loophole when it comes to employment as well. The Catholic school system, even though it is constitutionally funded by taxpayers in most provinces, belongs to a church that denounces *Charter* interpretations that recognize discrimination protection for queer people. They are also protected by that *Charter* under freedom of religious expression sections. Little Flower Academy, for example, has a potentially legitimate legal argument if it were to say that Lisa Reimer was fired because her lesbianism goes against the school's religious belief system. It is up to judges to negotiate this contradiction in the *Charter*, and this could lead to problems in future, particularly if Stephen Harper continues to stack the court system with like-minded individuals.

Queer-Positive Content and Policy in Schools

In 1972, British Columbia MPP George Mussallem rose in the provincial legislature in outrage over learning a representative of the "gay liberation movement" had been allowed to speak at a high school in New Westminster, B.C., announcing that education about homosexuals had no place in the school system.[18] Forty years later, it often still doesn't. There have been exceptions, and while each exemplifies the valiant efforts of many people working within school boards, they once again make clear the greatest enemy of acceptance of queer people and issues in the education system: social conservatism.

One example came in spring 1992 in Ontario, when John Campey, an openly gay member of the provincial NDP caucus, held a meeting with the Toronto Board of Education. From recommendations from the school board's Lesbian and Gay Employees Group, Campey asked the board to approve a sexual orientation curriculum document that had been in the works for six years, to repeal a clause prohibiting the "proselytization of homosexuality" that had been board policy since 1981 and finally to establish a consultative committee on the education of gay and lesbian students, modelled after similar committees for Native and Black students. There was serious opposition. The *Toronto Sun* called the Toronto board "lunatics" who were "brainwashing our kids" and "promoting homosexuality." The Christian fundamentalists came out in full force, with Ken Campbell's Christian Freedom Party taking out an ad in the *Globe and Mail* asking Canadians to rise up against "the perversity of this gay/lesbian propaganda." Meanwhile, an allegedly "secular" group called Citizens United for Responsible Education (CURE) created a handbook full of distorted "scientific information" about gays and lesbians and advocated therapy to "cure" homosexuals (hence the acronym).[19]

But as Tim McCaskell, a board employee and an advocate for queer rights in the education system, writes in *Race to Equity*, Campey cleverly framed homophobia "as one more piece of the equity agenda both for the NDP caucus and the board."[20] He also mobilized queer students, parents and board employees to come out to meetings and put pressure on the board to deal with the issues. As a result, every one of his motions passed by the end of June.

In 1996, the Calgary Board of Education would provide another pioneering example, despite facing remarkable adversity from Alberta's Christian right. The board developed an information package to ensure the safety of sexual minority youth in their school district. Recommendations in the package ranged from workshops on homophobia and homosexuality being held for principals, counsellors and teaching staff to the suggestion that video material on the matter be purchased. This was more progressive than the provincial education board's initiatives even ten years later. As the package — named the Action Plan on Gay/Lesbian/Bisexual Youth and Staff Safety — reached the stages of final approval, the aforementioned right-wing magazine *Alberta Report* and various churches organized gatherings to discuss "the effects and ramifications" of the initiative. This led to the formation of a Calgary chapter of CURE, which aggressively mobilized conservative Calgarians to fight against the package. Their intimation led board members and staff at the

Calgary Board of Education to fear for their safety, necessitating a security checkpoint to get into the offices. But in the end, the board still unanimously adopted the policy.

Another leading organization in the fight for queer content and policy was the B.C. Teachers Federation (BCTF), which over-whelmingly approved the creation of a program to "eliminate homophobia and heterosexism in the B.C. public school system" in 1997. However, the outcry from the Christian right actually led to a notorious example of another anti-queer element in the history of Canada's education system: book banning.

The questionably named Citizen's Research Institute (CRI) distributed 10,000 copies of their "Declaration of Family Rights" to persuade parents to pressure schools and school boards against BCTF's program and hold public forums in a number of communities. Among them was Surrey, a community particularly supportive of CRI as six of the seven trustees on the community's school board were linked to Christian right (one of whom was the director of CRI). Shortly after BCTF announced the program, the Surrey Board of Education fought back by banning three queer-positive books that Surrey teacher James Chamberlain introduced into his kindergarten class: *Asha's Mums, Belinda's Bouquet* and *One Dad, Two Dads*.[21] They said the books dealt with "a sensitive and contentious matter inappropriate to children aged five to six" and that they would be "potentially offensive to the various cultural and religious groups in the region."[22]

This led to a seven-year battle that cost Surrey taxpayers over $1 million and found its way to the Supreme Court of Canada. The court would rule against the school board's argument that the books were unsuitable for children, saying the "children could not learn tolerance unless they are exposed to views that differ from those they are taught at home."[23] However, the decision didn't oblige any board to be more inclusive to queer-positive material. And in general, serious steps were still not being taken on provincial levels, or at least not steps that were being implemented. In the late 1990s and through

The Triangle Program

In the spring of 1995, the Toronto Board of Education's human sexuality counsellor Tony Gambini came up with the idea of a school for gay and lesbian youth modelled after New York's Harvey Milk program. He'd spent years watching as gay and lesbian students struggled to get an education in the secondary school system due to rampant homophobia from their peers. So why not offer a school where openly queer staff would deliver curriculum stressing gay and lesbian history and culture? The proposal became known as the Triangle Program.

By the time it opened, Mike Harris's Conservatives had taken power in Ontario and the political complexion of the whole province had changed. If the Triangle Program had been proposed just a short time later, it very likely never would have been launched. But with ten students, one teacher and one social worker, the Triangle Program began in September 1995 in one room at the Metropolitan Community Church in Toronto. Many of the students were troubled youth coming to Toronto from smaller communities around the province.

Initially, the program focused on Grades 9 and 10, with an emphasis on transitioning students back into more conventional high schools afterwards. But by the mid-2000s, the program saw more trans-identified youth coming into the program, and program teacher Jeffrey White said he felt more apprehensive about finding them a safe space after Triangle. So Triangle expanded to offer the entire high school program. By 2010, forty-three students were enrolled.

The program exists in large part due to the Toronto queer community. The school board pays for the teaching staff, the social workers and a small operational budget, but the vast majority of funding comes from community fundraising and sponsorship. This helps offset costs that most high schools wouldn't have to contend with, such as an extensive nutrition program. White explained that the majority of Triangle's students live on their own with limited personal budgets, so ensuring they receive food is key.

"If we didn't have that community support, we wouldn't exist," White said. "That's where a lot of community-based alternative schools fall by the wayside. They just can't raise the funds. So God bless our LGBTQ community. They do care, and they are able to raise the funds."

Source: Jeffrey White, interview, 2010. To learn more about the program, see <http://www.triangleprogram.ca>.

the 2000s, governments, school boards and teacher's organizations would enact various policies or set up various programs, but the majority of schools would not adopt them.

In a 2010 article in *Xtra!* that suggested the Canadian education system is "failing queer youth from B.C. to Newfoundland," Ontario elementary school teacher Ellen Chambers Picard said that schools and school boards are fearful of a backlash if they address queer issues in the classroom.[24] British Columbia, meanwhile, despite having one of the most queer-positive governments on education issues, has had significant problems in trying to execute their new initiatives.

In 1999, queer activists Peter and Murray Corren filed a human rights complaint against the British Columbia Education Ministry for "omitting their existence from the curriculum," which led to an agreement with the B.C. government to introduce a pioneering new queer issue–oriented elective course called "Social Justice 12," as well as the promise that "regular curriculum reviews" would be conducted with "an eye to the possibility of incorporating queer content." However, since the government did not make it mandatory, many school boards have been reluctant to offer the course. One in particular, the Abbotsford School Board, withdrew the course in 2008 despite the fact that student interest and enrolment were high. The government did not intervene, though student protests led to the school board reinstating the course under the provision that students "obtained parental consent" to take it.

That situation is unfortunately downright progressive compared to the recently passed Bill 44 in Alberta. Implemented in June 2009, the Act gave parents the right to pull their children out of class when lessons on sex, religion or sexual orientation are being taught. The Act was an amendment to the province's human rights legislation, and was initially intended to enshrine "sexual orientation" as a protected class from discrimination. It ended up doing so, but with it came a buried, contradictory clause that suggested parents have the right to shield their children from positive discussion of the very thing the bill was attempting to protect.

Queer Bashing and Homophobic Bullying

Within some of the more progressive policies touched upon so far in this chapter lie the beginnings of what is drastically needed in Canada's education system: protection for students from homophobic harassment. While the inclusion of a queer-positive curriculum is definitely an important goal, it does not address the need to protect queer students from emotionally and physically violent homophobia in schools.

Queer bashing and homophobic bullying among youth — in schools, or anywhere else — is not a new problem but in the past decade or so, it has been a problem of increasing visibility.[25] For one thing, major queer-organizing groups have taken up the cause with a passion that was definitely not present pre-2000. For example, after same-sex marriage became an officially resolved issue, EGALE Canada — the country's only national lobbying group — started attending to school issues.[26] But also, the increase in mainstream acknowledgement of queer issues has led to a drastic rise in visibility among queer youth themselves. The average coming out age has dropped drastically in the past decade, which makes homophobic bullying a much more pressing issue than in the past. It also presents a generation of queer teenagers with the challenge of openly asserting their queerness within the school environment. Take Jeremy Dias, who filed a complaint with the Ontario Human Rights Commission in 2002 when staff members at his school — Sault Ste. Marie's Sir James Dunn Collegiate and Vocational School — refused to allow him to start school clubs to encourage a queer positive environment. He settled out of court with the school board and used the money to start the Jeremy Dias LGBTQ Scholarship Fund, an endowment fund for high school and CEGEP grads.[27]

A 2009 study by EGALE Canada has made it clear that things are not easy for queer youth today. Key findings in the study — the first National Climate Survey on Homophobia in Canadian Schools — included that 75 percent of queer students felt unsafe in at least one place at school, while 60 percent had been verbally harassed and another 25 percent physically harassed. The study also concluded that teachers or school officials have not proven significantly helpful. Fewer than a fifth of the students in the survey said the staff at their schools intervened "always or most of the time" when they heard anti-queer comments, and fewer than half of participants in the survey even knew whether their school had a policy for reporting homophobic incidents. Of those who did know, only a third believed there was such a policy.[28] Sadly, those numbers seem quite accurate. Generalized anti-discrimination and harassment measures were enacted by school boards in the late 1980s and early 1990s, but as with queer-positive curriculum, they were accompanied with little to no discernable action. By the 2000s, more action was being taken, but there were significant problems.

The Ontario legislature, for example, approved the *Safe Schools Act* in 2001, which dramatically increased the penalties for bullying and violence. However, it did not specifically target homophobic bullying and violence, nor were they the catalyst for this legislation. It came rather in response to school shootings — notably at Columbine High School in Littleton, Colorado, on April 20, 1999, and W.R. Myers High School in Taber, Alberta, on April 28, 1999. In both cases, bullying was said to have triggered the teenage gunmen.

Around the same time, pressure on officials in British Columbia became very much about homophobic bullying and violence. In 2000, a high school student in Surrey named Hamed Nastoh committed suicide, leaving behind a note that clearly blamed the action on homophobic taunting. "Please tell the school why I did this," the note said. "I don't want somebody else to have to do what I did."[29] Soon after Nastoh's death, the provincial auditor general recommended that measures be taken to assist in doing just that, but things did not move along very quickly. In 2002, the Safe School Task Force was established, but a report by them a year later made absolutely no recommendations on how to combat homophobic bullying. In 2004, the provincial education ministry released guidelines on school safety regarding harassment and violence, but queer-specific examples were not included. In 2005, an openly gay Liberal MPP entered a "safe schools" bill into the legislature that did include sexual diversity, but it was defeated.

British Columbia was also the site of the first case in Canada that charged school officials with responsibility for bullying, testing how far the *Charter* could really go in terms of protecting queer students. North Vancouver's Azmi Jubran became fed up with the inaction by school officials regarding the homophobic harassment and threats he had been receiving for years, despite the fact that he identified as heterosexual (this is actually much more common than one would think). Jubran took his case to the B.C. Human Rights Commission, where in 2002 they ruled in his favour. They rejected "school official arguments that they could not be held responsible for the conduct of students, stating that schools had an obligation to provide an environment free from discrimination and harassment, and that failure to do so was discriminatory."[30] But the school appealed the ruling to courts, where they won because Jubran was not a homosexual, and thus the Human Rights Code's prohibition on anti-gay discrimination did not apply. Thankfully, the B.C. Court of Appeal later upheld Jubhan's claim and ruled that "the school board had to adopt a proactive and broad educative approach to such issues as harassment, homophobia and discrimination."[31]

In the midst of this, students themselves started to claim visibility. Gay-straight alliances (GSAs) — student-run groups that promote queer positivity among all students — began to form in the late 1990s and early 2000s, and proved an excellent tool in creating safe spaces within education institutions. Alberta's first GSA formed in 2000 in Red Deer, noted as "the centre of religious conservatism in an already conservative province."[32] In 2004, half of Vancouver's public schools had GSAs, and by 2006, the Canadian Teacher's Federation issued a handbook on the development of GSAs, which helped facilitate their sharp increase across the country. However, this development has not been embraced by Catholic school boards. In February 2011, an article in *Xtra!* revealed that GSAs were banned from all Ontario Catholic school boards, where the taxpayer-supported school system's understanding of sexuality was determined by its religious leaders, not the policies of the Ministry of Education.[33] The boards were instructed that all their teachings and programs must be informed through the *Pastoral Guideline to Assist Students of Same-Sex Orientation*, which on the one hand calls for the elimination of "practices like bullying and unjust discrimination," and on the other states that if a student is "suffering" from same-sex attractions, they must never act on them. It reads, "The bottom line of church teaching on gay sexual activity is simply: Don't. Ever. This is called lifelong abstinence, or a celibate lifestyle."[34]

As Catholic school boards continue to refuse to align themselves with the relative progress of the public system, incidents exposing the tragic potential of homophobia continue to occur. In 2007, high school student Shaquille Wisdom from Ajax, Ontario, killed himself as a direct result of homophobic bullying. This is not an isolated case. Suicide is the leading cause of death among queer youth, who account for about 30 percent of all successful suicide attempts.[35] But in 2010, awareness of this skyrocketed, largely due to the suicide of Rutgers University student Tyler Clementi. Clementi was an eighteen-year-old who jumped to his death after his college roommate video-streamed over the internet a sexual encounter Clementi had with a man. The incident gained remarkable mainstream attention in the United States, and this spilled over into Canada, in large part thanks to the American-initiated viral video campaign "It Gets Better."

The "It Gets Better" campaign published hundreds of queer-positive messages on YouTube that appealed to youth to "hang in there, because adult queer life offers much more opportunity for progressive environments" (these messages often came care of celebrities and politicians, including American president Barack Obama and British prime minister David Cameron; Canada's Stephen Harper did not participate). The message of the videos presented a questionable compromise for the harsh reality of queer youth, and did not advocate for the more ideal situation of things "getting better" for youth more immediately. But they did create a considerable dialogue, including in Canada. Tommy Smythe, who co-founded a Canadian spinoff of the "It Gets Better" series, joined University of Toronto professor and queer academic David Rayside, EGALE President Helen Kennedy and Susan Magerman of Toronto's Triangle Program on TVOntario's program *The Agenda* to discuss issues surrounding the "It Gets Better" series. They quickly asserted that, contrary to widely held opinion, the Canadian situation is not much better than it is south of the border. "We have the statistics," Helen Kennedy said on the show. "We know the extent of the problem. Now we just need to make sure we take the responsibility to do something about it."[36] Rayside was quick to acknowledge that politicians were not proving capable of Kennedy's request. "During the same-same marriage debate, there were some pretty powerful statements made in favour of same-sex marriage [from politicians]," he said. "But on this issue I think mostly what we've seen is some action on the school board level — there's no question about that — but mostly political hesitation."[37]

Some hope on that end has occurred in the past few years. In 2007, Canada's Human Rights Commission report on homophobia called for all schools — including religious ones — to engage in campaigns to combat homophobia, training for all school personnel on issues related to sexual diversity and more inclusive curricula in faculties of education. The move led Rayside to suggest in 2008 that what may result with regard to policy in education institutions is "a pattern reminiscent of policy change in the recognition of same-sex relationships — not particularly ahead of the curve by Canadian standards, but wide-ranging once it comes."[38]

So far, Quebec has been the only province to really fall in line with Rayside's prediction, introducing a comprehensive, province-wide campaign against homophobia in December 2009 that set an international precedent for inclusive policy, not just with regard to education institutions, but in every realm. According to the Quebec justice ministry's website, "La Politique québécoise de lutte contre l'homophobie" — as the campaign is called — is part of a "broader strategy leading to the full and complete recognition of sexual minorities, institutional and community support for sexual minorities, and improved knowledge about sexual diversity."[39]

One can only hope that Quebec's step forward will trickle down to other provinces soon, unlike when it took nearly a decade for a second province to follow its human rights legislation. But even if it does, we've seen time and again that policies don't always result in societal change. This will not put an end to heterosexism or institutionalized homophobia in Canadian society, not just among youth, but also with regard to all queer people. Violent homophobia is not exclusive to youth. Homophobic hate crimes rose over 50 percent in 2008 compared to 2007 but nearly 75 percent of such crimes still go unreported.[40] Schools were the second most likely environment for these crimes to occur, and while that is substantial and frightening, it still leaves a lot of ground to cover outside of the education system.

6. HEALTH

There is an extensive history around queer people and health institutions. Historically, the term "homosexuality" emerged as a medical condition during the 1890s, when Richard von Krafft-Ebing's book *Psychopathia Sexualis* referred to homosexuality as a "physiologically based psychiatric pathology" attributed to a congenital weakness of the nervous system.[1] The medicalization of homosexuality provides a nightmarish and shocking narrative — with drugs, electroshock treatments, aversion therapy and even lobotomies being used to "cure" gays and lesbians — that precedes the chronology of this book.

By the late 1960s, psychiatry began to adopt relatively tolerant views toward homosexuality and the treatments noted above became rarer (in large part, due to years of activism). The American Psychiatric Association, in recognition of scientific evidence, finally removed "homosexuality" as a mental disorder in 1973, stating, "Homosexuality per se implies no impairment in judgment, stability, reliability, or general social or vocational capabilities."[2] But this simply suggested homosexuality should be tolerated as a second-class form of sexuality and by no means put an end to the problematic relationship queer people have had with health issues and institutions. This post-medicalization period will be discussed in this chapter.

HIV/AIDS will certainly be a dominant focus. It devastated communities and re-medicalized gay men, allowing mainstream society to associate them aggressively with disease and death. Its history in the Canadian context is remarkable, horrifying and greatly untold. It is a history that reaches across the country and affected thousands of individuals, each of whom have their own story. The discussion here is a mere introduction and suggestions for further learning are listed at the end of this book.[3] HIV/AIDS, of course, is *not* the only health issue facing queer people, despite the fact that it seems to be only one that gets substantial attention, particularly in the mainstream. A broad range of issues, largely being ignored, continues to threaten queer people.

HIV/AIDS: A Historical Canadian Overview

The first mention of what would eventually become known as HIV/AIDS came in the United States in June 1981, when a report from the Center for Disease Control was picked up by both mainstream and queer media. The report described five cases of severe pneumonia that involved young gay men, notable because the illness — pneumocystis carinii pneumonia (PCP) — occurred almost exclusively in newborn babies or people who were taking immunosuppressive drugs.

The first Canadian case was reported in the March 27, 1982, issue of *Canada Diseases Weekly Report*. A gay man in Windsor, Ontario, had entered the hospital on the fifth of January that year, dying six weeks later. He had been diagnosed with PCP (people did not die from AIDS itself, but from a range of diseases, like PCP, brought on by the repression of the immune system caused by HIV infection). By the fall of that year, there were fourteen cases in Canada (versus 625 in the U.S.). Forty-one percent of those cases had already resulted in death. Though gay men were certainly not the only affected group — Haitians and hemophiliacs were at risk — they made up the vast majority of cases.[4]

From that point on, the queer community and the queer rights movement were both altered dramatically. Theoretically, Canada gained a certain advantage given that the emerging AIDS epidemic was two years behind the United States. But there was almost no preparation carried out in medical institutions and public health departments. All that work was done by dozens of extraordinary people faced with something catastrophic. "The organized gay community across North America needs to be preparing for the 'health crisis' onset when it leaves Manhattan, as it has already begun to do," Michael Lynch wrote in a November 1982 *Body Politic* article. "Surely we must, as a community, continue to improve our educational referral efforts. As in gay health care over the past decade, our intent must not be to frighten or to moralize, but to inform and care."[5] It quickly became clear how necessary this would be. By September 24, 1984, the number of cases in Canada had grown from 14 to 105. By December 31, 1986, there were 830 cases; 683 were gay men, and 339 were already dead.[6]

The first actions were to launch social service organizations. Vancouver had the first forum on AIDS in March 1983, and AIDS Vancouver was born out of it. The AIDS Committee of Toronto (ACT) followed shortly thereafter. By the end of 1985, the Manitoba Gay Coalition had held a forum, the Montreal AIDS Resource Centre formed out of the Gay Montreal Association, Halifax had created a Gay Health Association, and Edmonton had its own AIDS network. This first round of organizing was to create places to do education work in the community as people began to understand that this was probably a communicable disease. But there was little overt political activism around AIDS, and the appalling response from federal and provincial governments was beginning to make this necessary. AIDS seemed to bring out some of the vilest homophobia the country had yet seen from public officials.

In Nova Scotia, the health minister had suggested quarantine for sexually active people with AIDS, while British Columbia had introduced a bill that would have given the government power to quarantine anyone suspected of testing positive for antibodies to HIV. Elected officials in both provinces genuinely considered designating islands off their coasts — former leper colonies — as the sites for quarantine. In Saskatchewan, the Canadian AIDS Society found a request for funding sent by an AIDS group to the Saskatchewan health minister. The document had been found in the minister's files with "Go to Hell" written on it.[7]

By 1986, drugs that were proving effective at treating the disease in other parts of the world were not being approved for use in Canada. Finally in Vancouver, where the provincial Social Credit government had been particularly unresponsive (despite being the province with the highest per capita AIDS cases in Canada[8]), the first treatment activism emerged, drawing largely on the activist traditions of the 1970s and early 1980s. The first AIDS protest in Canada — held on March 26, 1986, on the steps of the legislature in Victoria — was staged by the newly formed Vancouver Persons With AIDS Coalition to demand a viral laboratory in the province. Even if people with AIDS found access to the necessary drugs, no lab would then allow doctors to monitor the blood samples. Sadly, even when the lab opened the following year, its existence did not lead to drug access.

Other groups followed Vancouver's lead. In late 1987, Montreal's Comité des personnes atteintes du VIH du Québec grew out of dissatisfaction with Comité SIDA Aide de Montréal (C-SAM), which was seen as "too focused on education and health issues."[9] Shortly after, AIDS Action Now! (AAN!) — the most influential and well-known Canadian AIDS activist group — started organizing. "We began to realize what was going on in the community," AAN! activist Tim McCaskell recalled. "There was all this frustration building up. People were still dying. There was no treatment or information about how to get treatment. You had organizations like the AIDS Committee of Toronto that were basically holding people's hands as they died."[10]

Inspired by New York's AIDS Coalition To Unleash Power (ACT

UP), AAN! would come to focus on the state of AIDS research and the availability of drugs. There was one drug in particular, aerosolized pentamidine, which had shown great progress in combating PCP. However, it was not legal in Canada. In the face of increasing demand for action, the drug eventually went to a national trial to test its efficiency (though it had already proved quite efficient in the United States), where 750 people across the country who had already had one bout of PCP volunteered to test the drug. Except that half of the people in the trial were to unknowingly take a placebo, which alarmed AAN! considerably.[11] "We weren't very sophisticated, but we knew Grade 10 math," McCaskell said. "You take 350 people who already had one bout of PCP and their likelihood of getting it again within a year. We knew the second bout of PCP was often much worse than the first, and what that death rate was. So we figured out they were basically going to kill 10 or 15 people in this trial to prove the drug worked, even though we had evidence from the U.S. that said it did."[12]

To combat the trials, AAN! built coffins and marched them down to Toronto General Hospital (one of the sites for the trial), vocally relaying the statistics they had calculated, and demanding the trial be stopped. The message got through. When Brian Mulroney's Progressive Conservative government (who were met with "Silence=Death" placards by AAN! whenever they campaigned in Toronto) were re-elected the following month, one of the first announcements made by the new health minister was that Canadians would now be able to access experimental AIDS treatments through the Emergency Drug Release Program (EDRP).[13]

The EDRP was set up to authorize the sale of drugs to a doctor for a specified patient when a medical emergency existed and standard therapy was not effective. In 1987–88, the EDRP had approved 7515 emergency drug releases, but none to treat AIDS or AIDS-related conditions.[14] Now, drugs including aerosolized pentamidine would be included in the program. The placebo trial was halted as a result, and a whole range of new treatments were made available.

The Montreal Manifesto

This is a shortened version of the Manifesto as it was read in Montreal on June 4, 1989, at the Palais de Congres before the opening of the International AIDS Conference:

This declaration sets forth the responsibilities of all peoples, governments international bodies, multinational corporations and health care providers to ensure the rights of all people living with HIV disease.

1. All governments and all international and national health organizations must treat HIV disease positively and aggressively as a chronic, manageable condition. Ensuring access and availability of treatment must be part of the social and moral obligations of governments to their citizens.

2. Government must recognize that HIV disease is not highly infectious. Casual contact presents no threat of infection, and irrational fears of transmission must be fought.

3. An international code of rights must acknowledge and preserve the humanity of people with HIV disease [list of specifics followed].

4. A multi-national, international data bank to make available all medical information related to HIV disease must be created. This includes all data concerning drug and treatments, especially basic bio-medical research and the initiation of any progress of clinical trials.

5. Placebo trials must be recognized as inherently unethical when they are the only means of access to particular treatments.

6. Criteria for the approval of drugs and treatments should be standardized on an international basis to facilitate worldwide access to new drug treatments.

7. International education programs outlining comprehensive sex information supportive of all sexual orientations in culturally sensitive ways and describing safer sex and needle practices and other means of preventing HIV transmission must be made available.

8. The unequal social position of women affecting their access to information about HIV transmission must be recognized and also their right to programs redressing this inequality, including respect for women's right to control their own bodies.

> 9. Industrialized nations must establish an international develop-
>   ment fund to assist poor and developing countries to meet their
>   health responsibilities including the provision of condoms,
>   facilities for clean blood supply and adequate supplies of
>   sterile needles.
>
> 10. It must be recognized that in most parts of the world, poverty
>   is a critical co-factor in HIV disease. Therefore, conversion of
>   military spending worldwide to medical health and basic
>   social services is essential.

By 1989, over 2500 Canadians had been diagnosed with AIDS, the vast majority of them gay and bisexual men. While there had been minor progress thanks to activist work, Ann Silverside notes in *AIDS Activist* that unlike many other industrialized nations, Canada had "no national strategy to combat the epidemic."[15] The Fifth International Conference on AIDS — to be held in Montreal that June — would be an opportunity for AIDS activists to help change that. In what was to be the largest gathering of researchers to discuss one of the most devastating diseases in the history of science, AIDS Action Now! and Montreal's Reaction SIDA teamed up with New York's ACT UP. They created "The Montreal Manifesto," also known as "The Declaration of the Universal Rights and Needs of People Living with HIV Disease," and together (though with a few disagreements), they took over the opening ceremonies at the Palais des Congres. Waving signs that read "Silence=Death" and "The world is sick of government genocide" as they entered the building, the groups then headed to the stage. Prime Minister Brian Mulroney was to open the conference with his first-ever public remarks on AIDS despite being prime minister since 1984. But before he could, the AIDS activists stormed the stage, and Tim McCaskell took the microphone and said: "On behalf of people living with AIDS in Canada and around the world, I would like to officially open the Fifth International Conference on AIDS."[16] McCaskell added that Mulroney's presence constituted "an unprecedented historical piece of political hypocrisy given the record of the Mulroney government on AIDS." Then the Montreal Manifesto was read aloud in both French and English, and, apart from politicians and drug companies, it was actually embraced by most of the conference attendees. When Mulroney finally came to speak, the activists (who had taken seats in the audience after they left the stage to no protest) stood up and turned their backs to him, undoing their wristwatches and holding them in the air to signal that time was indeed running out.

The stories behind AAN! and similar groups across Canada are multitudinous and astonishing and paved the way for a relatively easier road to victories in the coming years. Through demonstrations and lobbying, drugs became available and affordable, and the government began to listen. For example, AAN! stormed another conference in 1994 — this time the NDP's Ontario provincial conference. After four years of promising a government-funded drug plan for people with HIV/AIDS, the NDP government had done nothing. So AAN! threatened Ontario Premier Bob Rae with being burned in effigy at a demonstration unless he approved the plan. In one of the final pieces of legislation to come out of that government (Mike Harris and the Conservatives were elected shortly thereafter), the drug plan was finally put in place.

HIV/AIDS Today

By 2000, a national AIDS Strategy was finally made permanent by Jean Chrétien's Liberal government, but by that point, HIV/AIDS had changed dramatically in how it was affecting people and which people were being affected. While drugs were extending and improving the lives of people with HIV exponentially, heterosexual women, black people and First Nations people had all become targeted risk groups, and the median age of those infected was dropping at an alarming rate. Perhaps due to this extension of demographics, the once small, volunteer-run HIV/AIDS organizations had become large bureaucracies with huge budgets from government grants and, increasingly, corporate sponsorship.[17] The concerns of men who have sex with men (or MSM, which has become the proper terminology with respect to HIV/AIDS as not all men who have sex with men identify as gay, bisexual or queer[18]) were becoming less dominant in these organizations, as was the kind of activism noted previously.

HIV/AIDS has not been cured and it still dramatically affects MSM. By the end of 2008, 51 percent of those living with HIV/AIDS (now exceeding 65,000) were MSM, according to a report by the *Canadian AIDS Treatment Information Exchange.*[19] That same report concluded that MSM also made up 47 percent of new infections in 2008, a number that has consistently risen over the previous decade. Even more alarming is a study of Canadian urban centres — Vancouver, Montreal, Ottawa and Toronto — that found that between 12 and 24 percent of MSM in those cities were HIV-positive (compared to the national average of 0.3 percent, in other words, approximately fifty times higher).[20]

With regard to HIV/AIDS and MSM, there are intersections involving other risk groups. For one, HIV/AIDS is increasingly becoming a disease of youth. A new generation of gay men who did not witness the horror of the 1980s are becoming more likely to practise unsafe sex, leading to a sharp increase in infection rates among MSM under the age of twenty-five. Racialized communities have also become more affected by HIV/AIDS. Groups specializing in these communities have existed since the 1990s, from the Black Coalition for AIDS Prevention (Black CAP) in Toronto to the Manitoba Aboriginal AIDS Task Force in Winnipeg to the Asian Support AIDS Group in Vancouver. While not exclusive to the queer community, many have roots in it. Queer activist Doug Stewart was instrumental in forming Black CAP, which is committed to dealing with "the impact of racism, sexism, heterosexism, homophobia, classism, and other forms of discrimination."[21] These groups address the specific concerns of intersections of queer and race identities that will be discussed further in Chapter 7. They are also necessary because,

Key Points Regarding HIV/AIDS and Men Who Have Sex with Men (MSM)

- HIV prevalence rates are estimated to range between 12 percent and 24 percent in MSM in five Canadian cities.
- The HIV prevalence rate in MSM is approximately fifty times higher in five Canadian cities than among the Canadian adult population.
- MSM continue to participate in sexual behaviours that place them at risk for contracting HIV.
- MSM accounted for 51 percent of all people living with HIV/AIDS in 2008.
- An estimated 47 percent of new HIV infections were in MSM in 2008.
- HIV incidence has been stable in MSM since 2005.

Source: "HIV in Canada: Trends and Issues that Affect HIV Prevention, Care, Treatment and Support." Canadian AIDS Treatment Information Exchange. December 2010 <http://www.catie.ca/pdf/canada/HIV-in-Canada_ES.pdf>.

as noted, HIV/AIDS has very much become a racialized disease, particularly regarding First Nations people. An estimated 4300 to 6100 First Nations people were living with HIV in Canada at the end of 2008, accounting for 8 percent of infections despite making up 3.8 percent of the population.[22] Another study, which looked at 576 full-blown AIDS cases involving First Nations people, saw that 30.6 percent of them were MSM. An additional 6.9 percent were MSM who also injected drugs.[23] That number is considerably less than that of the general population as this study saw 69.2 percent of non-First Nations people fall into the MSM exposure category.

Cases regarding First Nations people have largely been associated with the overwhelming degree of poverty affecting those communities. HIV/AIDS has become significantly associated with poverty in general, in large part due to dramatic changes in Canadian society. After the 1980s, a neoliberalist worldview was set in place, and numerous social supports from welfare to employment insurance to pensions were drastically reduced, increasing poverty among people with HIV/AIDS.

A 2006 study by Ontario-based Positive Spaces, Healthy Places conducted 600 interviews across the province and found that 75 percent of people living with HIV/AIDS were living below the poverty line.[24] "On the one hand, if you're too sick to work and end up on disability benefits, you're below the poverty line," Tim McCaskell noted. "Then on the other hand, we know poverty itself is a social determinant of health, so you're more likely to be infected if you're poor… In this neoliberal world, poverty doesn't unite people, it divides them. So if you're well-off and have a good medical plan, then you're not poor, whether you've got AIDS or not. And you're probably living pretty well, because the drugs work pretty well."[25]

Like Canadian society, the social division of the queer community has dramatically altered since HIV/AIDS began. Advances in rights in general gave certain members of the community relatively remarkable privilege, and access to that privilege has a lot to do with race and class. "Back in the early 1980s when we were all dying —

TABLE 5 Comparison of selected exposure categories for reported AIDS cases and positive HIV test reports (from provinces that report data) among First Nations and non-First Nations persons

	First Nations	Non-First Nations
AIDS Cases (1979–2006)	n=576	n=15,275
IDU*	39.9%	7%
Heterosexual	19.4%	15.5%
MSM	30.6%	69.2%
MSM/IDU	6.9%	4.4%

* injection drug user

n = number of cases with available information on exposure category

Source: "Aboriginal Strategy on HIV/AIDS in Canada II," *Canadian Aboriginal AIDS Network*, March 2009 <http://www.2spirits.com/>.

whether you were rich or poor or black or white — everybody was in the same boat," McCaskell said. "So that produced this real symbiosis across class and race and brought people together to produce a really powerful movement. But now we're in different boats and they are drifting further and further apart."[26]

As the fight against AIDS becomes increasing segregated, there's increasing need for unity. In August 2010, AIDS Action Now! — which had been largely dormant for most of the 2000s — held a community meeting reinvigorate the HIV, Hepatitis, Harm Reduction activist voices. As one would expect, the people in attendance were radically more diverse across race, class, gender and sexual orientation than when AAN! began.[27] But the obstacles discussed were all too familiar. Under Stephen Harper, the Canadian federal government was once again fuelling the fire of the HIV/AIDS epidemic.

A five-year Canadian AIDS strategy called "Leading Together" was to be completed in 2010. Enacted just prior to Harper taking office, the strategy was intended to increase awareness of HIV/AIDS, increase the commitment to sustained funding for HIV/AIDS programs and services, step up prevention efforts, and enhance "the front-line capacity to act early and stay the course."[28] But during Harper's term the government has pulled significant money out of "Leading Together," and has reneged on promises of increased funding while infection rates have risen 14 percent.[29]

A large concern at the AAN! meeting was how Canada's next national AIDS plan will be funded and implemented with a government that has actively denied the rights of people living with HIV, as well as those most affected: MSM, people living in poverty, people who use drugs, Aboriginal people, young people and newcomers to Canada. Through a combination of "grass-roots activism, public demonstrations, lobbying, collaborative work with other community organizations, research, and related activities," AAN! declared at that meeting that they would work to do the following:

1. Improve access to treatment, care and support for people living with HIV/AIDS in Canada and around the world.
2. Fight for effective HIV/AIDS prevention that respects human rights.
3. Work to improve the social determinants of health for communities struggling against the AIDS epidemic.[30]

These goals echoed some of what was demanded in the "Montreal Manifesto," which over twenty years after being proclaimed, remains largely unrealized.

Other Queer Health Issues

Health with regard to the queer community has predominantly focused on HIV/AIDS, but a broad range of other health issues are in dire need of attention. But a book this size unfortunately provides yet another example of how they are often lumped into one category of "not HIV/AIDS." This is largely because the issues are indeed quite broad, many of them affecting certain fragments covered under the queer umbrella. But the sum of the parts of these issues is sizeable and disconcerting. It is estimated that even without factoring in HIV/AIDS, queer people have a significantly lower life expectancy than the general population.

"We have the one of the poorest health status of any population in the country," said Gens Hellquist, executive director of the Canadian Rainbow Health Coalition (CRHC). "It's considerably higher than the general population, but it doesn't get addressed."[31] This arises because Canada largely has a health system that isn't equipped to deal with queer people. Health professionals get little or no training about queer health issues. Doctors might get training on HIV/AIDS, but if that is the only queer-focused training they get, it could potentially lead them to believe that this is the only serious health issue affecting queer people.

The situation regarding funding isn't helping matters either. Ed Jackson, a long-time queer activist and director of program development at Canadian AIDS Treatment Information Exchange (CATIE), explained that the funding pots are quite rigid when it comes to issues beyond HIV/AIDS. "While there's money going to HIV and AIDS, funders often don't know how to deal with these broader health issues," he said. "They can stretch it to sexual health but once you get into these broader health issues they say, 'well, you can't come to us with all this stuff.' They don't identify that there are queer communities across the country that need to be addressed in specific ways."[32]

Some of the issues include rates for suicide, smoking, substance abuse and mental illness that all substantially exceed the general population (especially for youth, as we saw in the previous chapter), as well higher rates of certain cancers (lesbians with breast cancer, gay men with anal and penile cancers) and a great susceptibility to homophobic violence. A 2003 literature review by CRHC estimated that more than 5000 queer Canadians die prematurely every year because of living in a homophobic environment.[33]

There's also the issue that MSM cannot donate blood or organs. Canadian Blood Services and Hema-Quebec both have policies that "indefinitely defer" acceptance of blood donations from "men who have had sex with men, even once, since 1977."[34] This has been in effect since March 10, 1983, and continues to send a clear and discriminatory message.[35] Recently, a case in Ontario saw Kyle Freeman attempt to challenge that the deferral policy as a denial of *Charter* equality rights. This came in defence of Canadian Blood Services suing Freeman for lying in response to the question of whether he had had sex with men. The Ontario Superior Court ruled against Freeman in September 2010.

With regard to the health concerns of queer people themselves, there are groups across the country working on a wide range of issues. Most urban areas have queer-focused health organizations, which began forming in the 1990s when it became clear they were necessary. For example, Saskatoon formed an organization in 1991 to work on broader health issues, such mental health issues, coming out and substance abuse. In British Columbia, the Lesbian, Gay, Bisexual, and Transgendered Health Advisory Committee was formed by the Vancouver/Richmond Health Board in 1997 to liaise with members of the community to define health issues and develop viable solutions. A similar group formed in Ottawa in 1999 to explore similar issues. Tom Warner said this activity suggested that "queer Canadians [were] fostering a new advocacy agenda that, by the early twenty-first century, showed signs of becoming a fully-fledged national movement."[36]

The founder of Saskatoon's group, Gens Hellquist, said he quickly became aware that there was little communication between the country's many groups, which led him to help organize the first national queer health conference in Saskatoon in 2001, where "The Saskatoon Declaration of GLBT Health & Wellness" was created. Out of the conference also came the creation of the aforementioned national group, Canadian Rainbow Health Coalition, with a mandate to educate and advocate around queer health issues across Canada.[37] But CRHC has run into problems lately. In January 2010 they filed a human rights complaint against Health Canada, alleging that they discriminate against queer people in their spending. In 2004, the CRHC had an annual budget of $2.3 million. Just five years later, it had shockingly dropped to just $10,000.[38] The mainstream media paid little attention to the complaint (still ongoing), and it didn't mobilize as strong a reaction from many people within the community as CRHC had hoped. Hellquist said this makes it clear that health issues aren't "sexy like same-sex marriage."[39]

Another issue that isn't proving particularly sexy is that of aging queer people. While working in Toronto's queer community Kristyn Wong-Tam, an activist since the late 1980s who in 2010 was elected to Toronto's city council, noticed that many older queers "took refuge in the village because it was relatively safe."[40] Gay seniors in mainstream institutions are finding the environment a little like being back in school because of the homophobia and the general anti-sex agenda of seniors' homes, and some have taken up activism again to combat this. "They wanted to build a sense of community, and they wanted to live amongst people who would understand," she said. "But now they're getting older and the apartments are getting more expensive. They're dealing with health issues, and I'm not talking about HIV or AIDS… it's just aging. Who checks up on them I don't know. But these are pioneers who took care of us. They may not even have social security or income security because they've dedicated so much of their lives to activism, which doesn't pay you anything. We have to get ready to take care of them. We have to build community intergenerationally. We have to plan for a community that's age-friendly. Putting multiple generations in the same room and sharing different experiences familiarizes one another with what we've gone through. It creates better understanding across generations."[41]

7. DIFFERENCE AND PRIVILEGE

In February 1977, the article "Divided We Stand" was published in the *Body Politic*. Written by Andrew Hodges, the article made clear the serious issue of difference and privilege within queer organizing, and it is one that resonates just as loudly today, if not more so. "In the conventional view, there are supposed to be 'people' who identify themselves as gay," Hodges writes. "Some just happen to be women, others men, just as some are black and others white. All alike are oppressed as 'gays' in this picture; all oppose the imposition of heterosexual values, all suffer discrimination or the threat of it, all are denied openness and spontaneity, all are alienated from the family system. In this model of the movement, all 'gay people' would put aside their differences (gender, race, class, and so on) to fight back. But this model failed as soon as it was invented."[1]

Canada — a state built on differences of class, gender, race, language and nation — has an international image of tolerance of diversity but racism, sexism and classism remain serious issues and play prominent roles in major issues surrounding the queer "community." Major battles have been won, but largely those battles have been won to serve a privileged group of queer people, more often than not those who are male, white and earn a middle-class wage or more. These also tend to be the people discussed in histories of queer Canada, even if they represent only portions of some of the letters in the "LGBTT" acronym, which stands for lesbian, gay, bisexual, transgendered and two-spirited. This book has purposely not utilized that acronym, instead opting for the less specific "queer," or when historically applicable, "lesbian and gay." The reasoning behind that is largely because for a book of this scope to take on an acronym so officially expansive is simply impossible.

The most crucial example is the history and issues surrounding transgendered people, who are not included in this book. There are considerable tensions and differences between transgendered people and those who identify as gay men or lesbians. Transgenderism is at its core an issue of gender identity, not queer sexuality, and as a social movement has not entirely coincided with the problems that have historically faced lesbians and gay people. This — alongside concerns that predominantly gay and lesbian-led groups will not make their specific issues a priority — is one of the main reasons why there has not been complete consensus among transgendered people as to whether they want to be part of the "LGBTT community." That said, gender and sexuality are in large part mutually constructed in Canadian society and broader queer oppression is certainly inter-related with gender oppression. Many authors discussing queer politics do include trans experience and struggles. But considering the length of this book, it did not seem fair to lump transgendered people in as a footnote to a movement that does not wholly represent them. Transgendered people deserve a book of their own. The works of Viviane Namaste and Dan Irving are excellent examples of just that.[2] This book, however, is not.

What this book has attempted to do is to speak to the history and issues surrounding Canadian queer sexuality as inclusively as possible but as a whole, gay white men are definitely prevalent. This is in part because their privilege has allowed them to play much more significant roles in the battles that have defined this history. But it is also crucial to understand the battles that have defined the less visible segments of queer sexuality in Canada. They may not have all been the dominant forces that led to human rights legislation or same-sex marriage, but they are the people largely left behind in its wake.

Lesbians

It may seem curious to group lesbians so generally within this chapter, particularly since some lesbians were indeed among the forces that led to human rights legislation or same-sex marriage. But the story of lesbian marginalization is quite significant, particularly in the early days of organizing when lesbians quickly realized that the initial model of the "gay rights movement" excluded them in many ways. Even its initial vocabulary focused on words like "gay" and "homosexual," which are both predominantly male-identified (the term "lesbian" became promoted and eventually accepted as the preferred term over "gay women" in the 1970s). Furthermore, "lesbian and gay" organizations were largely controlled by men and their definitions of the issues and solutions.

"Events done in the name of 'lesbians and gay men' are done almost entirely by gay men who invite lesbians to make up numbers in a fashion redolent of Victorian chivalry," Andrew Hodges noted in the article quoted at the beginning of this chapter.[3] Lesbians became fed up with the inability for any understanding that they were oppressed in different ways than their male counterparts. As it turned out, sexism did not disappear simply because the men were gay. This led them to a second avenue for organization: the feminist movement. Miriam Smith describes lesbian feminism in *Lesbian and Gay Rights in Canada* as "rooted in radical feminism and explicitly [challenging] the compulsory heterosexuality of the patriarchal system." Their goal was "the creation of a political and social identity, a necessary task given the oppression of women and the almost complete invisibility of lesbians in society and public life."[4]

However, the larger feminist movement wasn't always willing to work toward the goals of lesbians either. In 1969, a radical feminist organization Toronto New Feminists formed, but failed to address the issue of lesbian oppression. When a few lesbian members protested this, they were expelled from the group. A year later, the Indo-Chinese Women's Liberation Conference was held in the city, and planned lesbian workshops were cancelled at the last minute because of tensions in the group about "the lesbian question."[5] It seemed that homophobia didn't disappear simply because women were feminists.

This left lesbians in a very difficult position and led some to revolt against both the gay liberation and feminist causes and into a lesbian separatist movement. In December 1971, a group of lesbians at the Community Homophile Association of Toronto (CHAT), self-named "The Cunts," announced that they were starting an independent lesbian group and demanded that the mostly male CHAT membership confront its own sexism.[6] "Dykes and faggots in CHAT shall share equally in decision making," they said in a written statement. "This means equalization at *all* official decision making levels, i.e., in the proposed constitution, executive, vice-chair and chair."[7] This suggested amendment never went through, and the women walked out.

In *The House That Jill Built: A Lesbian Nation in Formation*, one of the greatest resources for Canadian lesbian history, Becki L. Ross explains that episodes like this "picked up steam and momentum as they reverberated across the country and resonated with the anger shared by increasing numbers of gay women and lesbian feminists."[8] In 1973, for example, the Women's Committee of GAY in Montreal decided to leave the group (which they found to be "overwhelmingly male in membership and outlook") and form Montreal Gay Women, a group that would publish *Long Time Coming*, the first strictly lesbian journal in Canada.

Though this lesbian separatist movement was quite vocal and an important part of Canadian lesbian history, it was viewed by most lesbians as extreme and impractical. Its ideology contemplated severely limiting involvement or even contact with heterosexual women and *all* men, and Ross explains that in the end most lesbian activists argued that collaboration outside the lesbian community was necessary. But this would not prove easy. Throughout the course of the 1970s, lesbians would continue to work with both feminists and gay liberation groups, but were often met with unsatisfactory or even hostile results, particularly from the latter.

The late Chris Bearchell, one of the most prominent lesbian writers for the *Body Politic* and an important figure in Canadian queer history, wrote the article "Gay Men and Lesbians *Can* Work Together" as a call to establish a relationship between lesbians and gay men. "Unity will only be forged when those few dykes who are in the gay movement can convince the movement as a whole to give priority to lesbian demands and struggles," she wrote. "Yes, lesbians have been burned by sexism in this movement. No, saying you're sorry won't make it better. Doing something on the other hand just might. Throwing full support behind a child custody fight, for instance, just might. We can't say for sure, because we haven't had the chance to try, yet."[9]

Bearchell also spoke passionately about the need for autonomous lesbian organizations, in that "while unity and the needs we share with gay men are political, not *all* lesbians' needs are [political]." These organizations would both serve the specific demands of lesbians, and work with gay and feminist organizations. By the mid-1970s, such groups would be present in essentially every major Canadian city, including the Lesbian Organization of Toronto (LOOT), Lesbians of Ottawa Now (LOON), Labyris Montreal, Calgary's Womyn's Collective and Edmonton's Womynspace.

There was also national organizing. The first exclusively lesbian conference — The Gay Women's Festival — was held at the YWCA in Toronto in June 1973. Fifty women from across the country attended. A year later, another conference sponsored by Montreal Gay Women saw more than 200 lesbian feminists attend, the largest gathering of its kind ever held in Canada.[10] Issues discussed at the events included legal rights, relationships, lesbian mothers, lesbians and employment and lesbian feminism.

There were definitely tensions within autonomous lesbian

organizing. Since so many lesbians ended up participating in such a wide variety of ideological frameworks — from lesbian and gay liberation to lesbian separatism to radical feminism — clashes were not rare. Issues regarding sexuality and censorship were particularly conflicting. Generally, heterosexual feminists were against things like lowering the age of consent and lax pornography legislation, while lesbian and gay liberationists often argued the opposite.[11] But despite this, this way of organizing has continued in a similar vein ever since. Into the 1990s and 2000s — though a bit more sporadically by this point — lesbians have found ways to negotiate a community outside their more visible and often more privileged gay male counterparts, as well as find one with them. Since 1986, Vancouver and Ottawa have held annual International Lesbian Week activities and, in 1996, Toronto first added a Dyke March to its Pride Week calendar, which has grown into a large event attracting over 5000 marchers. As of 2011, it is no longer specific to lesbians, but all women in what Toronto Pride deems the "LGBTTIQQ2SA" community (Lesbian, Gay, Bi-Sexual, Transsexual, Transgender, Intersex, Queer, Questioning, 2-Spirited and Allies).

As in the queer community as a whole, this new era of rights has brought a huge variation in privileges within that acronym for queer women, even if they are subject to sexism that queer men don't face. But issues are much more complex now than in the 1970s, as the diversity of the visible queer community — whether men or women — has expanded exponentially.[12]

Two-Spirited People

"Two-spirited" is a contemporary term that covers a wide range of identities. It emerged in 1990 from the third annual Inter-Tribal Native American/First Nations Gay and Lesbian Conference in Winnipeg (where the first ever powwow for queer Aboriginal people was held). Essentially, it describes queer First Nations people, many of whom believe that their body simultaneously houses both a masculine and a feminine spirit. It is a translation of the Ojibwa phrase "niizh manidoowag," and was chosen to distinguish queer First Nations people from their non-Native counterparts.[13]

On the website for the Toronto-based organization Two-Spirited Peoples of the First Nations, it is explained that historically, two-spirited people were looked upon as a "third gender in many cases and in almost all cultures they were honoured and revered." They were often thought of as visionaries, healers and medicine people, and were respected as a "fundamental component of ancient culture and society."[14]

European colonization destroyed many traditions and assimilated First Nations people into white, Christian culture. Non-Aboriginal values were taught as superior to First Nations values and, in the process, many First Nations people adopted homophobic attitudes. This has, coupled with alarming issues facing the First Nations community to begin with (from vast racism to extremely high rates of suicide, disease and homelessness), historically made being queer and Native complicated and challenging. Tom Warner writes in *Never Going Back* that in the early years of gay and lesbian organizing, racism present from Canadian society in general, as well as from underground gay and lesbian networks at the time, "dominated the lives and shaped the identities of the few Native women and men courageous enough to assert a same-sex orientation during this period."[15]

In the past few decades, two-spirited people have been organizing to support one another and to educate their community though it has not always come easily. In 1986, the Nichiwakan Native Gay and Lesbian Society was formed in Winnipeg, the first of its kind. However, by the early 1990s, it proved unsustainable and folded. Two Spirit Circle Society of Edmonton (TSCE) also has suffered from staff burn-out and not enough resources, though it does continue as of 2011.

One the most successful efforts came in 1989, when Art Zoccole and Bily Merasty formed the aforementioned Two-Spirited Peoples of the First Nations in Toronto, which also remains active. The group's goals are to provide a space for two-spirited people to meet and reclaim their traditions. They provide counselling, produce information and education on HIV/AIDS and publish an extensive website full of resources. "We Are Part of a Tradition: A Guide on Two-Spirited People for First Nations Communities," was written by Gilbert Deschamps in 1998 as part of Two-Spirited Peoples of the First Nations' mission. "We, as the two-spirited community, must heal," Deschamps writes in the guide, available in full on the organization's website. "We must re-learn that to be two-spirited is an honour. We have grown up with the single message that lesbians and gay men are sick. We are in the process of rebuilding a positive self-image as a result of this past. And if, as in the larger First Nations community, Two-Spirited people suffer from suicide, substance abuse, and short life spans, then we must recognize this as a symptom of a very different illness."[16]

A 2001 survey of 189 queer First Nations people asked which social factors had "negatively affected" their lives. Over 30 percent answered yes to "physical abuse," "HIV discrimination," "homophobia" and "suicide," while over 40 percent said the same to "poverty," "racism" and "poor housing."[17] Nearly a decade later, these issues all remain prominent, and they were discussed at length during a 2010 conference of two-spirited people held in Winnipeg, where approximately 100 people attended from across North America. A study from the University of Manitoba was presented that had conducted thirteen individual interviews and three focus groups with twenty-four two-spirited individuals. Among other things, the study emphasized the continuing impact of colonization, racism and homophobia on many two-spirited people's lives and recommended a need for "visible and accepting services in cities and in First Nations and Métis communities to address the specific needs of Aboriginal Two-Spirit and LGBTQ peoples." The entire study, as well as other extensive resources regarding two-spirited people, is available on the website of Two-Spirited Peoples of the First Nations.[18]

Queers of Colour

Like two-spirited people, the wide variety of racial and ethnic identities that fall under the heading "queers of colour" have their own sets of issues and often their own unique forms of marginalization. Including them all in one section is reductive in this sense, but given that different racial and ethnic queer groups have largely self-identified as "queers of colour," and that the narratives of these groups' emergence is somewhat similar, it seemed fair to do so given the scope of this book. They also often face a similar "cultural schizophrenia," as Asian-Canadian queer theorist and video artist Richard Fung explained in 1980:

> Non-white gays and lesbians face a double-edged sword: the racism of the general society as filtered into the gay community and the sometimes-vicious sexism and homophobia of our own 'ethnic' communities. These two factors alone have kept us isolated. The latter has prevented many from participating fully in our own community or if we do, it enforces a secretiveness that leads to cultural schizophrenia.[19]

This double-edged sword of oppression (or triple, for queer women of colour) has placed Canadian queers of colour in a challenging position within the queer spectrum, and one their white counterparts have often not been receptive to. Early organizing was overwhelming white and, just as the gay men in the movement were often adverse to the issues facing lesbians, the wide range of additional issues that queers of colour faced because of the marginalization of their race was not being addressed. This led queers of colour to have difficulties negotiating themselves into the movement, which was only enhanced by the individual racism on the part of many white members in the lesbian and gay liberation movement of the 1970s, as well as the organizing that came after that.

"When I came out I knew that I wanted to be part of a community that was going to be inclusive and compassionate and forward-thinking," Asian lesbian activist Kristyn Wong-Tam noted of trying to negotiate her identity as a woman of colour in the queer community of the late 1980s and early 1990s. "And I think that the LGBT movement, the way I came out into it was not those things. There were some fringes around what the gay rights movement could do and say for us, but there weren't enough diverse voices at the table to feed into the quest for policy change or the quest for charter changes."[20]

Those kinds of issues would lead to self-organization on the part of queers of colour, what Gary Kinsman deems "one of the first challenges to a unitary lesbian, gay, and even queer identity."[21] Beginning in the 1980s, queers of colour started organizing across Canada to deal with both the racism and homophobia they experienced. The first was Gay Asians of Toronto (GAT), formed by Richard Fung and Gerald Chan in 1980. Among the purposes of the group were "promoting unity and mutual support among gay Asians; organizing social, cultural, educational, and recreational activities for its members; providing culturally sensitive social and support services; and advocating on issues relevant to their community's concerns."[22]

The first Black queer group also started in Toronto, with Zami, founded in 1984 and named after an East Caribbean word for lesbian sex. Doug Stewart, one of the group's original organizers, was one of the first people in the Toronto community to speak out publicly against the exclusion and racism that queers of colour faced from the overall queer community. In a 1986 letter to the *Body Politic*, Stewart said that racism among gay men, "forces gay men like me to prioritize my concerns… Black gay activists define themselves first and foremost as Black and as gay second."[23]

The letter came in the midst of much anger from queers of colour in the Toronto community after the *Body Politic* had published an advertisement from a white gay man who was seeking a "young, well built BM [Black Man] for houseboy."[24] The ad resulted in a meeting between the *Body Politic* and representatives of Zami, GAT and recently formed Lesbians of Colour. According to a letter GAT's Alan Li wrote to the *Body Politic* shortly after the meeting, things did not go over well. "[It was] one of the most unpleasant meetings I have ever attended," Li said in a letter directed at the *Body Politic*'s largely white, male, middle-class staff. "We were made to feel that our arguments were non-representative, and our objections hysterical, and our feelings defensive… Women and third-world gays have added battles to fight because of the fact that we are at the other end of the power differential. To us, racism, sexism, and socio-economic as well as political oppression are equally important issues to be confronted."[25]

The reasons for Li's anger were reasonably widespread across many communities in Canada, and organizing continued. By the 1990s, there were groups like Asians and Friends in Ottawa, Gay Asians and the Long Yang Social Club in Vancouver, Gais et lesbiennes asiatiques in Montreal, Of Colour in Calgary and Juka, the Nova Scotia Black Gay, Lesbian and Bisexual Association in Halifax. In addition to fighting racism in the white male-dominated queer community, these groups also had to fight against heterosexism and homophobia in their racialized community. In 1996, a Toronto Rastafarian newspaper ran an article that called "homosexualism" a "depraved crime against humanity."[26] That same year GAT lashed out against a Toronto Chinese-language newspaper that said it was "unavoidable to have a phenomenon of hatred, contempt, and discrimination towards people afflicted with homosexuality."[27]

There were also conflicts *within* queers of colour organizing. Besides Toronto's aforementioned Lesbians of Colour, Winnipeg, Ottawa, Calgary and Vancouver were among the cities to have women-specific groups. "The level of oppression that one has to deal with if they happen to be women of colour, and happen to be queer, and — God forbid — happen to be butch women or transgendered is exceptional," Kristyn Wong-Tam noted. "These are compounded layers of societal hatred… So we saw this splintering of women's organizations that said 'we're going to organize this way, because the way the men were organizing didn't allow space for women's voices.' There was some collaboration when it came time to work on common issues. But at any given time when I look across the decades when I've done some of this work, the best work was done when women were at the table."[28]

Wong-Tam also noted divisions when it came to class, and that issues affecting women and lesbians of colour are often socio-economically related. "If the only people sitting around the table were middle-class white men, then the only things we'd be asking for would benefit those who come from that demographic," she said. "But then if you throw poor, racialized lesbians of colour into the mix, the quest becomes broader."[29]

There were also instances when everyone did try to work together. Queer Nation — a short lived but extremely high-energy activist movement in the early 1990s — focused in large part on a rejection of the assimilationist activism of the 1980s, and on the intersecting forms of oppression that faced many queer people.[30] Allan Bérubé and Jeffrey Escoffier described Queer Nation as "trying to combine contradictory impulses: to bring people together who have been made to feel perverse, queer, old, outcast, different, deviant, and to affirm sameness by defining a common identity on the fringes."[31] Queer Nation brought a renewed sense of militancy to activism, and essentially rejected the identity politics and labels of the lesbian and gay movement, claiming that "labels such as gay, lesbian, bisexual and community promoted by now mainstream activists were intended to integrate, homogenize, and make respectable those who were once sexual outlaws."[32] It started in New York City in April 1990 and chapters opened in Toronto, Ottawa, Vancouver and Montreal within a year.

Though it attempted to be inclusive to all queer people and fight oppression of all forms, Queer Nation was often criticized for actually marginalizing those whose didn't conform to the new "nation." It also was accused of being dominated by white males and for not dealing with racism in the way it had originally suggested it would.

Tom Warner explains that many queers of colour drawn to Queer Nation's profession of inclusiveness "drifted away because their voices got lost in the frenzy of mostly white, mostly male meetings."[33]

Queer Nation was doomed to last only a couple of years in most places due to a lack of organizational sustainability. Autonomous organizing for queers of colour, meanwhile, continued and in the 2000s began expanding to accommodate the growing number of different racial and ethnic groups due to an influx in immigration in Canada from an expansive group of countries.

But Alan Wong, who has worked with queer Asian groups in Montreal and also helped organize La coalition MultiMundo, which brings together various queer ethnic and racial groups in Montreal, said that keeping these groups going is a huge challenge. This has been true since the beginning of this organizing, with groups often only lasting a few years. But the economic situation of the mid-to-late 2000s — and the fact that queer organizations often have to rely on sponsorships instead of government funding (which is less of a problem for moneymaking events like Pride) — made this even worse. "We don't get sponsorships," Wong said. "They don't see us as benefiting them, as we're so small. We're a sub-group of a sub-group in their eyes. And getting money from not-for-profit sources? That's the next step where everybody goes to for money. So all these people are competing for the same funds from the same people. So it's become really difficult."[34]

But this organizing remains necessary. The combined marginalization of race and sexual orientation is a lot for people to negotiate without community support, and this is especially true for youth. However, Wong said that his experiences working as an activist in the post same-sex marriage world has made clear a feeling of being "left behind" by a larger queer movement now that certain rights have been achieved. "Something that's critical that a lot of people are forgetting in the community is why they came there, and how they got there, and what it took to get there. Now that they've gotten a certain amount of privilege, they're forgetting. So now what I think the community needs to do is be self-reflexive, and to remember those times when they were struggling to get those rights that they have now. Because there are still people in their community who are trying to get those rights as well, and they are calling on their queer brothers and sisters to help them achieve those particular goals. But ultimately seeing backs turned on them."[35]

Immigrants, Refugees and Migrants

According to the Canadian government, Canada has the highest per capita immigration in the world.[36] In the 2000s, the makeup of that immigration largely included Latin Americans, Middle Eastern Arabs and South Asians — all areas of the world where homosexuality is often outlawed with serious penalties. With those immigrants has come a wave of queer people, many of them refugees or refugee claimants escaping brutally homophobic societies that make the situation described in this entire book look ideal by comparison. This brings a new set of issues to the table, ones not being given the attention they need.

Over 40 percent of new immigrants settle in the Toronto area, where Suhail Abualsameed, a community worker and activist who immigrated to Canada from Jordan, has been working with immigrant and refugee queer youth at Supporting Our Youth (SOY). In 2002, Abualsameed and SOY started a five-month project to bring together queer immigrants and refugee claimants, who, despite Toronto's demography, were not very present at SOY. The project — called "Express" — targeted youth between sixteen and twenty-nine who were newcomers to Canada, refugees, refugee claimants and non-status queer and trans youth. Most of the participants are young people coming from countries or cultures where it's not safe, legal or easy to be queer.

Abualsameed said he quickly started to hear stories of youth trying to attend more generalized queer youth programs in Toronto but facing discrimination based on their poor English, their fashion or other culturally specific traits. "They felt more alienated in the queer community than they did anywhere else," Abualsameed said, "which is horrible. So we realized we needed this safe space to feel comfortable not speaking a language very well or feel comfortable with their refugee label. They also just need to feel like their story has value. Most of the kids have valuable stories of coming out and homophobia in their homes, but being someone who is actually running away from a country or a person who wants to kill them is different than kids at school bullying or bugging them sometimes."[37]

The project turned into a full-time program, which continues to this day. In a typical group of twenty youth, Abualsameed said ten different languages and ten different countries are represented. Some had just arrived in Canada a week prior and had never spoken to a queer person in their life, while others had been coming to the group for some time. The majority of them are refugee claimants, and the program works to help them achieve refugee status.

Since the early 1990s, Canadian refugee practice and policies have allowed people fearing persecution related to sexual orientation or gender identity (SOGI) to become Convention Refugees in Canada. While a progressive move in itself, it has been bogged down with a number of factors that have made SOGI-based claims challenging. For example, refugee verdicts are decided by a single person, which leaves the door open for homophobia to affect what is truly a life-or-death decision. Bill C-291, which would have created a Refugee Appeals Division to hear cases that had been rejected, died on third reading when Parliament was prorogued in December 2009.

Another bill, Bill C-11, passed in June 2010, did create the Refugee Appeals Division but it also reformed the immigration and refugee system to fast track certain refugees and make it faster to deport others. This would result in a list of "safe countries of origin," meaning that claimants that come from "safe" countries would be denied access to the Refugee Appeals Division. Janet Dench, executive director of the Canadian Council of Refugees, explained that the bill would lead to certain refugees "being denied the protection that they need, and particularly there are certain categories of refugees that, from experience with the current system, we know would be particularly vulnerable under a system like that because they may be claims that are successful from countries that otherwise are seen as being democratic and quite peaceful."[38]

Dench said claims related to SOGI were among the most vulnerable, which Abualsameed and a network of other queer activists across the country clearly agree with. Among them are Sharalyn Jordan and Chris Morrissey of Vancouver, who have been working on queer immigration issues since the 1990s. Jordan and Morrissey initially worked with the group LEGIT: Canadian Immigration for Same-Sex Partners, which took on cases where non-Canadian partners of queer Canadians sought to gain access to the country. But when they started to get more and more requests for assistance around asylum issues where people needed to make refugee claims because of the persecution of their sexual orientation or gender identity, they formed Rainbow Refugees, a separate group to deal specifically with these issues.

Rainbow Refugees worked hard in the fight against the problematic elements of Bill C-11, preparing a report to present to the Standing Committee on Citizenship and Immigration that details the impact of the bill on refugee claimants who have survived sexual orientation or gender identity persecution. "Canada has a critical role to play in providing a place of safety for those whose lives, safety and rights are at risk due to persecution of their Sexual Orientation or Gender Identity," the report reads. "We urge the Standing Committee on Citizenship and Immigration to be cognizant that their decisions on Bill C-11 have consequences for the lives and Human Rights of all potential refugees, and to recognize the particular challenges of LGBT refugee claimants."[39]

The report concluded with key principles of a "fair, effective, fast and efficient refugee system that will serve to protect those making SOGI based claims," which ended up being realized to a degree through the advocacy of Rainbow Refugees and other groups. The "safe list," for example, was all but written out of the final version of the bill but other issues remained. Claimants still face the possibility of being forced to a hearing after just sixty days, leaving them little time to put together documentation that makes clear their dire situation.[40] "We experienced success in some of the most problematic aspects of the bill being changed," Jordan said. "But there are still many problems with this legislation. It's going to be implemented over the next few years, and we'll be watching how that affects the rights of queer applicants."[41]

While programs like Rainbow Refugees and Express are incredible resources for immigrants, migrants and refugees, and help bring forth a sense of community for them, inclusion in the rest of society — including by queer people — remains problematic. Queer people from other countries have unique histories, and with them come specific forms of sexual oppression and marginalization that many other Canadians fail to recognize. An event that puts into context some of these issues arose when, in 2010, Toronto Pride banned the group Queers Against Israeli Apartheid (QuAIA) from marching in their parade under that name. Many queer people believed that Toronto Pride's decision (which was reportedly influenced by the City of Toronto and other major funders of Pride) went against their community's solidarity with all struggles of oppression. After considerable protest on behalf of QuAIA and its supports, Pride took back the ban. But the signification remained, setting a very dangerous precedent for the exclusion of certain political perspectives within queer movements and communities.[42]

"When Pride Toronto says you can walk in the parade, but you can't use these words and you can't bring your politics from your own country with you, that is a very symbolic thing of what's happening in our community," Abualsameed explained. "It says that if you are to be accepted, you need to assimilate. If someone from Palestine comes to Canada, they come with the fact that their inability to be openly queer before coming to Canada had a lot to do with the Israeli occupation and the politics of the Middle East. To

The following are the key principles suggested in "Rainbow Refugee Committee Responds to Bill C-11 on Refugee Reform" for a fair, effective, fast and efficient refugee system that will protect those making SOGI-based claims. The report was prepared for the Standing Committee on Citizenship and Immigration in May 2010.

- Good, independent decision makers: Recognize the importance of selecting and retaining decision makers in a manner that retains their independence, and train them well. Invest in developing training and guidelines on SOGI-based claims.
- Fair hearings: Recognize the high level of trauma and stigma that SOGI-based claimants may have experienced, and the ways that it may interfere with interacting with officials. Recognize that the conditions under which claimants provide testimony impacts the quality of evidence they are able to provide. Ensure that protocols for vulnerable persons can be followed at each step of the process.
- Equal access: Accord each claimant equal access to a hearing and an appeal. Refugee decisions should never rest in the hands of a single individual.
- Recognize that homophobic and transphobic violence and social intolerance are complex, changing and cause very real harms: Invest in gathering good country condition evidence. Allow consideration of Humanitarian and Compassionate grounds when there are potential risks that do not meet the definition for Convention Refugee protection.

For full document see: Christine Morrissey, "Rainbow Refugee Committee Responds to Bill C-11 on Refugee Reform," *Rainbow Refugee Committee*, May 2010 <http://www.parl.gc.ca/Content/HOC/Committee/403/CIMM/WebDoc/Rainbow%20Refuge%20Cmte%20E.pdf>.

come and tell people that we don't want to acknowledge that this is just 'a celebration of being gay'… this is not right. And you often see something similar when Latin Americans come from countries dealing with drug wars and corruption and they come here and nobody gets what's happening."[43]

Cultural clashes — as we've seen throughout this chapter — are nothing new in the history of queer Canada. Canadian queer culture is very white, somewhat understandably so. "It was created by a white culture," Abualsameed said. "These people fought a lot to create the gay rights movement, which is great. But then is that going the same speed as the immigration culture and the multicultural scene in Canada? Is that adapting to this? And the answer is a big 'no.'"[44]

However, one of the most important things to keep in mind is that some white gay people — even middle-class men — *do* understand this. Many people leading this resistance movement against what Pride was doing and what Bill C-11 was doing were white people. This chapter isn't meant to villainize all of the more privileged queer people (or heterosexual people, for that matter), but instead seeks to speak to that privilege and promote an understanding of how privilege and difference have marginalized many segments of queer people. But in the end, the greatest hope is that all people — no matter what sexual orientation, gender, race or class — can understand one another and work together to fight against the oppressions produced by the larger society that are clearly trickling down and creating a hierarchy within the queer community. "We need to work with each other and mentor each other and understand each other," Abualsameed said. "We need go to beyond that whole 'immigrant victim' versus 'evil, powerful white person' narrative. That's not helping anyone, and it's not true."[45]

8. WHERE DO WE GO FROM HERE?

Compared to the Canada of the 1970s, where queer activism emerged, the country has clearly seen drastic and far-reaching changes. Yes, those changes do indeed include many positive ones for the many queer Canadians, as this book has chronicled. But the question raised at the beginning of this book remains: What do these changes mean? Hopefully it is now clear that they have not meant equal rights for all queer people. There's a notion in this fight for queer rights that the jewel in the crown of equality is same-sex marriage. But this notion does not take into account that the background to the picture of queer rights has been changing fundamentally. Canada has been changing. Its cultural makeup has changed remarkably, as the last chapter explained. It has also changed from the liberal welfare state that lesbian and gay liberation was born into to the neoliberal capitalist nation that it is largely today. This has altered the context in which the queer movement operates, and has led to race and class disparities within the queer community that have been exasperated and amplified. In turn, we've seen the benefits to the gains that have been won become more and more unequally distributed.

This privileging permeates Canadian society, but there also remain many issues specific to the queer community. Homophobia and heterosexism remain dominant, both officially — such as in the Canadian education and health systems — and even more so unofficially. Canada is still very much an inherently homophobic and heterosexist society, as has been exemplified in everything from social conservative groups to violent queer bashers. And these opponents of making Canada a truly queer positive place do not necessarily discriminate. Hate remains directed toward all queer people: urban and rural, black and white, rich and poor, young and old. It may be exponentially easier for the more privileged to avoid the situations and environments where this occurs, but that shouldn't make them so complacent in coming together with all queer people to address the problems that *should* personally concern them.

Once same-sex marriage was legalized, mobilization suddenly deflated significantly, and organizations began to struggle financially. The country's longest running liberation group, CLGRO, dissolved in January 2009 for a variety of reasons including a considerably dwindling membership and the fact that there was no longer a coalition of groups, as most activist groups no longer exist. EGALE saw its annual operating budget go from $538,000 at the peak of the marriage debate to just $160,000 in 2009.[1] It seems that even though issues unquestionably remain on the table, many happily married same-sex couples aren't interested in taking them on.

But there are definitely still people who are taking them on, and that's not a reference to corporate-sponsored Pride events. It's a reference to groups like Queers Against Israeli Apartheid, noted in the previous chapter for standing up to Pride when it tried to censor its political perspective, or groups like Queer Ontario, one of the projects that came out of CLGRO's demise. With a mission of "challenging and seeking reform to social norms and laws that regulate queer people," it has a somewhat different character than previous activist groups in its clear intention to utilize online social media to mobilize communities.[2]

It's also a reference to the people who have lent their voices to the pages of this book, and the many people like them. They are unwilling to accept the relatively progressive situation that queer

Canada has now compared to the days when lesbian and gay liberation pioneered the fight for the rights that many of us might take for
granted. And they have the spirit of those very people, even if they
face a very different Canada that economically makes grassroots
activism and organizing more challenging than ever, even if socially
and politically it's quite the opposite. But there are ways, and it often
starts with simply becoming informed.

A group of queer people in Montreal did their part by putting
together a booklet called *Queers Made This* in the summer of 2010.
Chronicling 2005 to 2010, the booklet intended "to document the
dynamic histories of queer resistance in Montreal for folks now and
in the future." It explained its reasoning:

> As younger radical queers in a large urban centre, it can be
> difficult to make connections to older generations of queer
> organizers and activists. Stories of queer resistance can
> be difficult to come by, or are focused on non-local events
> like the Stonewall riots. Rather than learning our histories
> from one another, we find them in obscure corners of the
> internet, or not at all.[3]

Throughout the process of reading this book, you have indeed
avoided succumbing to such ignorance. And it should only be the
beginning. The history and issues expressed here are mere introduc-
tions that can be expanded by reading the books or watching the
films noted in this book, by visiting the lesbian and gay archives in
Toronto and Montreal, or by connecting with older generations of
queer people who have important perspectives and stories to share.
"If you believe in liberation, then it can't stop with you," said one
person. "It can't stop with you personally, and it can't stop with you
once you're married and have a dental plan. That's just a sham."

ENDNOTES

Chapter 1: What Does Our Progress Mean?

1. Gary Kinsman, *The Regulation of Desire: Homo and Hetero Sexualities* (Montreal: Black Rose Books, 1996), p. 25.
2. Gary Kinsman, "Challenging Canadian and Queer Nationalism," *In a Queer Country: Gay & Lesbian Studies in the Canadian Context*, Terry Goldie, ed. (Vancouver: Arsenal Pulp Pres, 2001), pp. 209–34.
3. Tom Warner, *Never Going Back: A History of Queer Activism in Canada* (Toronto: University of Toronto Press, 2002), p. 13.
4. Warner, *Never Going Back*, p. 10.
5. Gays of Ottawa, *Understanding Homophobia*, leaflet, 1975.
6. Warner, *Never Going Back*, p. 13.
7. Kinsman, *The Regulation of Desire*, pp. 33–34.
8. While the entire collection of the *Body Politic* is available at the Canadian Gay and Lesbian Archives in Toronto, an anthology of select articles was compiled for *Flaunting It! A Decade of Gay Journalism from The Body Politic*, Ed Jackson and Stan Persky, eds. (Toronto: Pink Triangle Press, 1982); Rick Bebout's remarkably extensive website is available at <http://www.rbebout.com/>.

Chapter 2: Regional Organizing

1. Donald McLeod, *Lesbian and Gay Liberation in Canada* (Toronto: ECW Press, 1996), p. 7.
2. As is the danger with introductory books such as this, the history of ASK is considerably more complex than noted in this paragraph.

Gary Kinsman describes the organization in *The Regulation of Desire*, pp. 229–48.

3. "Gay Alliance Toward Equality (Vancouver)" vertical file, *Canadian Lesbian and Gay Archives*, Toronto.

4. McLeod, *Lesbian and Gay Liberation in Canada*, p. 189.

5. Robert Cook, "350 Demand End to Police Harassment," *Body Politic*, May 1977.

6. Interview, Michael Phair, 2010.

7. McLeod, *Lesbian and Gay Liberation in Canada*, p. 72.

8. Interview, Gens Helquist, 2010.

9. Interview, Stephen Lock, 2010.

10. Ibid.

11. "London Group Makes Plans for New Centre." *Body Politic*, September 1974.

12. Gerald Hannon, "Anatomy of a Sex Scandal: What Happened in Ottawa," *Body Politic*, March 1976.

13. McLeod, *Lesbian and Gay Liberation in Canada*, p. 111.

14. "Rage! Taking It to the Streets," *Body Politic*, March 1981.

15. Interview, Gerald Hannon, 2010.

16. Interview, Tim McCaskell, 2010.

17. Harry Sutherland's 1982 documentary *Track Two* chronicles the raids and is a fascinating resource on understanding this time in Toronto history. It is available in full online.

18. Two excellent resources — and authors — for further exploring of queer history from a Quebec-specific perspective: Line Chamberland, *Mémoires lesbiennes: le lesbianisme à Montréal entre 1950 et 1972* (Montréal: Remue Ménage, 1996); Ross Higgins, *De la clandestinité à l'affirmation: pour une histoire de la communauté gaie montréalaise* (Montréal: Comeau and Nadeau, 2000).

19. Ron Dayman. "Quebec: First Five Years of the Movement," *Body Politic*, December 1976.

20. Interview, Ross Higgins, 2011.

21. Dayman, "Quebec: First Five of Years of the Movement."

22. McLeod, *Lesbian and Gay Liberation in Canada*, p. 110.

23. "Olympic Crackdown," *Body Politic*, August 1976.

24. Ibid.

25. "Thousands take to streets in protest," *Body Politic*, December/January 1976/1977.

26. Interview, Robin Metcalfe, 2010.

27. For a more in-depth look at rural issues, see Michael Riordan, *Out Our*

Way: Gay and Lesbian Life in the Country (Toronto: Between the Lines, 1996).

28. "Saskatchewan Gay Coalition," *Body Politic*, February 1978.

29. Phillip Fotheringham, "Rural Outreach: 'What? Gay People Here?'" *Body Politic*, April 1982.

30. Warner, *Never Going Back*, p. 311.

31. Riordan, *Out Our Way*, p. xi.

32. Miriam Smith, *Lesbian and Gay Rights in Canada: Social Movements and Equality-Seeking, 1971–1995* (Toronto: University of Toronto Press, 1999), p. 95.

33. Interview, Alan Wong.

Chapter 3: Law Reform

1. Jeffrey Weeks, *Coming Out: Homosexual Politics in Britain from the Nineteenth Century to the Present* (London; Quartet Books, 1977), pp. 106–7.

2. Warner, *Never Going Back*, p. 19.

3. McLeod, *Lesbian and Gay Liberation in Canada*, p. 13.

4. Warner, *Never Going Back*, p. 46.

5. McLeod, *Lesbian and Gay Liberation in Canada*, pp. 41–42.

6. Kinsman, *The Regulation of Desire*, p. 159.

7. George Smith, "In Defence of Privacy: Or, Bluntly Put, No More Shit," *Action! Publication of the Right to Privacy Committee*, 3, 1.

8. "We Demand" was a brief presented to the federal government in August 1971. Written and researched by Toronto Gay Action, it was supported by gay organizations across Canada. On August 28, 1971, over 200 people rallied on Parliament Hill in support of the brief. The action was the first of its kind in Canada. For the complete document, see "We Demand: The August 28th Gay Day Committee," *Body Politic*, November/December 1971.

9. "Labour Minister Responds," *Body Politic*, February 1973.

10. "City Bars Job Discrimination," *Body Politic*, November 1973.

11. Warner, *Never Going Back*, pp. 148–49.

12. John Moreau, "Gay Rights Back on Manitoba's Agenda," *Body Politic*, July–August 1984.

13. Michael Riordan, "The End of the Human Rights Decade," *Body Politic*, July 1979.

14. Smith, *Lesbian and Gay Rights in Canada*, pp. 91–92.

15. Interview, Michael Phair, 2010.

16. Warner, *Never Going Back*, p. 209.

17. Interview, Michael Phair, 2010.

18. Gloria Filax, *Queer Youth in the Province of the "Severely Normal"* (Vancouver: UBC Press, 2006), p. 160.

19. Interview, Gerald Hannon, 2010.

20. David Rayside, *Queer Inclusions, Continental Divisions* (Toronto: University of Toronto Press, 2008), p. 4.

21. For more on CLGRO's attempt at forging a consensus regarding relationship recognition, see Warner, *Never Going Back*, pp. 218–35.

22. William Walker, "Same-Sex Rights Bill Will Go to Free Vote," *Toronto Star*, 11 May 1994.

23. For a more detailed account of this narrative, see Kinsman, *The Regulation of Desire*, pp. 313–17 and Warner, *Never Going Back*, pp. 232–34.

24. Kinsman, *The Regulation of Desire*, p. 313.

25. Warner, *Never Going Back*, p. 239.

26. "Harper vs. the Globe and Mail," *Globe and Mail*, 6 September 2003.

27. Ibid.

28. SES Research Poll, 8 September 2003 <http://www.sesresearch.com>.

29. "Alberta gives in to same-sex marriage," *Xtra!*, 21 July 2005.

30. Interview, Ed Jackson, 2010.

31. For an expansion on these issues, see Law Commission of Canada, *Beyond Conjugality: Recognizing and Supporting Close Personal Adult Relationships* (Ottawa: Law Commission of Canada, 2001).

32. For a more extensive take on this issue, see Brenda Cossman, *Bad Attitude/s on Trial: Pornography, Feminism, and the Butler Decision* (Toronto: University of Toronto Press, 1996).

33. McLeod, *Lesbian and Gay Liberation in Canada*, pp. 103–4.

34. "TBP Raided and Charged," *Body Politic*, February 1978.

35. Alan Orr, "Sex Is Okay — If It's Not Gay," *Body Politic*, September 1986.

36. Warner, *Never Going Back*, p. 275.

37. Aerlyn Weissman, *Little Sister's vs. Big Brother*, documentary (National Film Board of Canada, 2002).

38. Paul Gallant, "The Honeymoon's Over: What's Next for the Gay Rights Movement?" *This Magazine*, September/October 2009.

39. Marcus McCann, "PG-rated gay film seized en route to Ottawa film fest," *Xtra!*, 21 November 2009.

40. For more on these cases, see Warner, *Losing Control: Canada's Social Conservatives in the Age of Rights*, pp. 99–100.

41. Interview, Brenda Cossman, 2010.

Chapter 4: Institutions

1. Kinsman, *The Regulation of Desire*, p. 34.
2. Kinsman, *The Regulation of Desire*, p. 264.
3. McLeod, *Lesbian and Gay Liberation in Canada*, p. 34.
4. The work of George Smith is a pivotal resource to understanding the *Criminal Code* and how it organized policing of queer sex. See George Smith, "Policing the gay community: An inquiry into textually-mediated social relations." *International Journal of the Sociology of Law*, 16, 1988, pp. 163–83.
5. Becki L. Ross, *The House That Jill Built: A Lesbian Nation in Formation* (Toronto: University of Toronto Press, 1995), pp. 47–48.
6. Gary Kinsman and Patrizia Gentile, *The Canadian War on Queers: National Security as Sexual Regulation* (Vancouver: UBC Press, 2010), p. 7.
7. Ibid.
8. Warner, *Never Looking Back*, p. 196.
9. See Smith, "Policing the gay community: An inquiry into textually-mediated social relations."
10. Eleanor Brown, "Male Cops at Pussy Palace," *Xtra!*, September 2000.
11. Matt Thomas, "First Person Account of the Toronto G20 Protests," *Xtra!*, 28 June 2010.
12. "We Demand: The August 28th Gay Day Committee," *Body Politic*, November/December 1971.
13. McLeod, *Lesbian and Gay Liberation in Canada*, p. 194.
14. "Gay couple awarded $13.4K for rent refusal," CBC News, 20 September 2010 <http://www.cbc.ca/news/canada/north/story/2010/09/20/yellowknife-gay-couple-landlord-ruling.html>.
15. McLeod, *Lesbian and Gay Liberation in Canada*, p. 162.
16. United Church of Canada <http://www.united-church.ca/history/overview/timeline#80>.
17. This was done through the "banns of marriage," a public announcement in a Christian parish church of an impending marriage. The publication of banns in Ontario remains a legal alternative to obtaining a marriage licence.
18. For an extensive exploration of the relationship between moral conservatism and the queer rights movement, see Tom Warner, *Losing Control: Canada's Social Conservatives in the Age of Rights* (Toronto: Between the Lines, 2010).
19. Interview, David Rayside, 2010.
20. Rayside, *Queer Inclusions, Continental Divisions*, p. 35.

21. Focus on the Family <http://www.focusonthefamily.com>.
22. "Thousands rally for same-sex marriage protest," *Catholic News Agency*, 12 April 2005.
23. Warner, *Losing Control*, p. 221.
24. Rayside, *Queer Inclusions, Continental Divisions*, p. 117.
25. Rayside, *Queer Inclusions, Continental Divisions*, p. 40.
26. Gareth Kirkby, "There was a Defence of Religion Act," *Xtra!*, 5 April 2007.
27. Ibid.
28. McLeod, *Lesbian and Gay Liberation in Canada*, p. 118.
29. Ibid.
30. Gerald Hannon, "Anatomy of a Sex Scandal: What Happened in Ottawa." *Body Politic*, February 1976.
31. Kinsman, *The Regulation of Desire*, pp. 336–38.
32. Joseph Woodard, "An AIDS cure could increase gay promiscuity," *Alberta Report*, March 1996; Joseph Woodward, "Winners and Losers: Why do Canada's courts invent charter rights for gays and not for babies?" *Alberta Report*, November 1997.
33. Andrew Brett, "Gays vs. the Toronto Sun," *Xtra!*, November 2010.
34. Ibid.
35. Donald McLeod chronicles the magazine in the book *A Brief History of Gay: Canada's First Gay Tabloid*.
36. Warner, *Never Looking Back*, p. 173.
37. Michael Riordan, "Five Years of *The Body Politic*," *Body Politic*, December/January 1976/77.
38. Interview, Chris Vogel, 2010.
39. For an extensive explanation see the final issue of the *Body Politic*, February 1987.

Chapter 5: Children, Youth and Education

1. Bruce MacDougall. "Silence in the Classroom: Limits on Homosexual Expression and the Privileging of Homophobic Religious Ideology," *Saskatchewan Law Review*, 1998.
2. Antonia Zerbisias, "Gay teens told it gets better, stats reveal crisis in our schools," *Toronto Star*, 5 November 2010.
3. For more on heterosexism in the school systems, see Didi Khayatt, "Compulsory Heterosexuality: Schools and Lesbian Students," *Knowledge, Experience and Ruling Relations: Studies in the Social Organization of Knowledge* (Toronto: University of Toronto Press, 1995); and George W. Smith,

"The Ideology of 'Fag': The School Experience of Gay Students, *Sociological Quarterly*, 39, 2, pp. 309–35.

4.   Rayside, *Queer Inclusions, Continental Divisions*, p. 167.

5.   McLeod, *Lesbian and Gay Liberation in Canada*, p. 176.

6.   Francie Wyland. "Lesbian Mothers," *Resources for Feminist Research*, March 1983, p. 41.

7.   Bruce MacDougall, *Queer Judgments: Homosexuality, Expression, and the Courts in Canada* (Toronto: University of Toronto Press, 2000), p. 116.

8.   Darryl Wishard. "Out of the closets and into the courts: Homosexual fathers and child custody," *Dickinson Law Review* 93, p. 430.

9.   Katherine Arnup, "Out in This World: The Social and Legal Context of Gay and Lesbian Families," *Gay People, Lesbians, and Family Values*, T. Richard Sullivan, ed. (Binghamton, NY: Harrington Park Press, 1999).

10. Rayside, *Queer Inclusions, Continental Divisions*, p. 186.

11. Brian Laghi, "Same Sex Marriage Bill Must Stand, Majority Say," *Globe and Mail*, 18 July 2005.

12. Rayside, *Queer Inclusions, Continental Divisions*, p. 187.

13. Peter Millard, "Assault on the Ivory Tower: Doug Wilson vs. the University of Saskatchewan," *Body Politic*, June 1976.

14. Rayside, *Queer Inclusions, Continental Divisions*, p. 232.

15. Ibid.

16. Ibid.

17. Jeremy Hainsworth. "Vancouver school fires lesbian teacher," *Xtra!*, 28 April 2010.

18. McLeod, *Lesbian and Gay Liberation in Canada*, pp. 93–94.

19. Tim McCaskell, *Race to Equity: Disrupting Educational Inequality* (Toronto: Between the Lines, 2005), p. 169.

20. Ibid.

21. Warner, *Losing Control*, pp. 199–200.

22. Ibid.

23. *Chamberlain v. Surrey School District No. 36*, [2002] SCC 86.

24. Natasha Barsotti. "How the Canadian education system is failing queer youth," *Xtra!* 28 January 2010.

25. For more, see Brian Burtch and Rebecca Haskell, *Get That Freak: Homophobia and Transphobia in High Schools* (Winnipeg: Fernwood Publishing, 2011).

26. It is notable that while EGALE did begin taking up issues surrounding schools, there has been significant criticism in the lack of consultation EGALE has done with other groups active around these questions.

27. James Moran, "Jeremy Dias creates scholarship with rights settlement," *Xtra! Capital*, 16 June 2005.

28. "Youth Speak Up about Homophobia and Transphobia: The First National Climate Survey on Homophobia in Canadian Schools," *EGALE Canada*, March 2009 <http://egale.ca/extra/CG_Taylor__Climate_Survey__Phase_One_Report.pdf>.

29. Rayside, *Queer Inclusions, Continental Divisions*, p. 230.

30. Ibid.

31. Ibid.

32. Ibid., p. 232.

33. Justin Stayshyn and Andrea Houston, "Catholic bishops prohibit gay-straight alliances in Ontario schools," *Xtra!* 11 February 2011.

34. Ibid.

35. "It Gets Better," *The Agenda*, TVOntario, 4 November 2010.

36. Ibid.

37. Ibid.

38. Rayside, *Queer Inclusions, Continental Divisions*, p. 241.

39. Barsotti, "How the Canadian education system is failing queer youth."

40. "Gay men targets of violence as hate crimes jump," *Toronto Star*, 24 June 2010.

Chapter 6: Health

1. R. von Krafft-Ebing, *Psychopathia Sexualis* (London: Velvet Publications, 1997).

2. J.J. Conger, "Proceedings of the American Psychological Association, Incorporated, for the year 1974: Minutes of the Annual Meeting of the Council of Representatives," *American Psychologist*, 30, 620–51.

3. A great start is watching the film and video work of John Greyson, and reading Ann Silversides' deeply personal and affecting *AIDS Activist: Michael Lynch and the Politics of Community* (Toronto: Between the Lines, 2003).

4. Ed Jackson, "Nationwide AIDS Report: Checking up on the Experts," *Body Politic*, July/August 1983.

5. Michael Lynch, "Living with Kaposi's," *Body Politic*, November 1982.

6. "AIDS: The Figures," *Body Politic*, November 1984; "Fighting For Life," *Body Politic*, February 1987.

7. Interview, Gens Hellquist, 2010.

8. Rob Joyce, "Still in the Waiting Room," *Body Politic*, June 1986.

9. Warner, *Never Going Back*, p. 252.

10. Interview, Tim McCaskell, 2010.

11. Ibid.

12. Ibid.

13. In addition to EDRP, these actions caused treatment arms of drug trials to be initiated.

14. Silversides, *AIDS Activist*, p. 185.

15. Ibid.

16. For footage from the events of that day, see John Greyson's 1989 video *World Is Sick (Sic)*. Greyson's *The AIDS Epidemic* (1987), *Angry Initiatives, Defiant Strategies* (1988) and *Zero Patience* (1993) are also very worthwhile explorations of AIDS in Canada.

17. For more on the transformation of community-based AIDS groups — which involves a rather complex process of state funding and regulation — see Gary Kinsman, "Managing AIDS organizing: 'consultation,' 'partnership,' and 'responsibility' as strategies of regulation," *Organizing Dissent: Contemporary Social Movements in Theory and Practice*, William K. Carroll, ed. (Toronto: Garamond Press, 1997) pp. 215–31.

18. The term was created in the 1990s by epidemiologists in order to study the spread of disease among men who have sex with men, regardless of identity.

19. "HIV in Canada: Trends and Issues that Affect HIV Prevention, Care, Treatment and Support," *Canadian AIDS Treatment Information Exchange*, December 2010 <http://www.catie.ca/pdf/canada/hiv-in-Canada_ES.pdf>.

20. Ibid.

21. Warner, *Never Going Back*, p. 255.

22. "HIV in Canada: Trends and Issues that Affect HIV Prevention, Care, Treatment and Support." *Canadian AIDS Treatment Information Exchange*.

23. "Aboriginal Strategy on HIV/AIDS in Canada II," *Canadian Aboriginal AIDS Network*, March 2009 <http://www.2spirits.com/>.

24. Sean B. Rourke, Jean Bacon and Ruthann Tucker, "Positive Spaces, Healthy Places: An innovative community-academic-policy partnership moves research into action," *Healthier Together: The CIHR Partnerships Casebook*. 2009.

25. Interview, Tim McCaskell, 2010.

26. Ibid.

27. Ibid.

28. "Leading Together: Canada Takes Action on HIV/AIDS," *Leading Together*,

2005 <http://www.leadingtogether.ca>.

29. "HIV in Canada: Trends and Issues that Affect HIV Prevention, Care, Treatment and Support."

30. "Constitution," AIDS Action Now! November 2010 <http://www.aidsactionnow.org/>.

31. Interview, Gens Hellquist, 2010.

32. Interview, Ed Jackson, 2010.

33. Julia Garro, "Canada's healthcare system is homophobic, says group," *Xtra!* 17 February 2009.

34. Eli Mills, "Blood rules discriminate," *Xtra! West*, 15 April 2004.

35. It is notable that this rule is certainly not exclusive to men who have sex with men. The dizzying list includes people who have lived in Africa, the Caribbean, England and France during certain times, those who work with monkeys and those who use IV drugs.

36. Warner, *Never Going Back*, p. 346.

37. For the complete Saskatoon Declaration of GLBT Health & Wellness document, see <http://www.avenuecommunitycentre.ca/pdf/resolutions.pdf>.

38. Interview, Gens Hellquist, 2010.

39. Ibid.

40. Interview, Kristyn Wong-Tam, 2010.

41. Ibid.

Chapter 7: Privilege and Difference

1. Andrew Hodges, "Divided We Stand," *Body Politic*, February 1977.

2. Specifically see Viviane Namaste, *Invisible Lives: The Erasure of Transsexual and Transgendered People* (Chicago: University of Chicago Press, 2000); Dan Irving, "The Self-Made Trans Man as Risky Business: A Critical Examination of Gaining Recognition for Trans Rights Trough Economic Discourse," *Temple Law Review*, May 2009.

3. Hodges, "Divided We Stand."

4. Smith, *Lesbian and Gay Rights in Canada*, p. 28.

5. Ross, *The House That Jill Built*, 24–25.

6. Ibid, 34–35.

7. McLeod, *Lesbian and Gay Liberation in Canada*, p. 86.

8. Ross, *The House That Jill Built*, p. 35.

9. Chris Bearchell, "Gay men and lesbians *can* work together," *Body Politic*, April 1977.

10. McLeod, *Lesbian and Gay Liberation in Canada*, p. 152.

11. This is a simplistic summary of a complex issue. It is not to say that there were not pro-sex feminists and feminists against censorship. For more on this issue see Brenda Cossman, *Bad Attitude/s on Trial: Pornography, Feminism, and the Butler Decision* (Toronto: University of Toronto Press, 1996).

12. For an incredible account of lesbian lives in Canada, watch *Forbidden Love: The Unashamed Stories of Lesbian Lives*, directed by Lynn Fernie and Aerlyn Weissman, 1992. The film interviews a number of women about their experiences of lesbian culture in Vancouver, Toronto and Montreal during the 1940s through the 1960s.

13. Jodi O'Brien, *Encyclopedia of Gender and Society* (Thousand Oaks, CA: Sage Publications, 1999), p. 64.

14. Gilbert Deschamps, "We Are Part of a Tradition," *2-Spirited People of the 1st Nations Report*, 1998 <http://www.2spirits.com/>.

15. Warner, *Never Going Back*, p. 34.

16. Deschamps, "We Are Part of a Tradition."

17. "Voices of Two-Spirited Men," *2-Spirited People of the 1st Nations Report*, 2001 <http://www.2spirits.com/>.

18. Janice Ristock and Art Zoccole, "Aboriginal Two-Spirit and LGBTQ Migration, Mobility, and Health Research Project," *2-Spirited People of the 1st Nations Report*, 2010 <http://www.2spirits.com/>.

19. Richard Fung, "Asians Gay and Proud," *The Asianadian*, Winter 1979–80.

20. Interview, Kristyn Wong-Tam, 2010.

21. Kinsman, *The Regulation of Desire*, p. 300.

22. Warner, *Never Going Back*, p. 75.

23. Doug Stewart, "Letters," *Body Politic*, May 1985.

24. "31 Words," *Body Politic*, April 1985.

25. Alan Li, "Letters," *Body Politic*, April 1985.

26. "Rastafari Takes Stand Against Homosexualism," *Uprising*, July 1996.

27. Marc A. Morrison, "Rightwingers Control the Media?" *Xtra!*, 29 August 1996.

28. Interview, Kristyn Wong-Tam, 2010.

29. Ibid.

30. Though included with the context of its connection to fighting racial oppression, Queer Nation was a considerably more complex movement than that. Its goals extended beyond simply queer-specific activism. For example, it also included anti-war activism against the Gulf War. See

Kinsman, *The Regulation of Desire*, 299–300; Warner, *Never Going Back*, 258–61; and Allan Bérubé and Jeffrey Escoffier, "Queer/Nation," *Out/Look*, Winter 1991 for further explanation.

31. Bérubé and Escoffier, "Queer/Nation."
32. Warner, *Never Going Back*, p. 258.
33. Warner, *Never Going Back*, p. 260.
34. Interview, Alan Wong, 2010.
35. Ibid.
36. "Immigration Levels Planning: Balancing Priorities to Meet Canada's Immigration Objectives," *Citizenship and Immigration Canada*, 2009 <http://www.cic.gc.ca/>.
37. Interview, Suhail Abualsameed, 2010.
38. Dale Smith, "Immigration reform bill could negatively impact queer refugee claimants," *Xtra!*, 31 March 2010.
39. Christine Morrissey, "Rainbow Refugee Committee Responds to Bill C-11 on Refugee Reform," *Rainbow Refugee Committee*, May 2010 <http://www.parl.gc.ca/Content/HOC/Committee/403/CIMM/WebDoc/Rainbow%20Refuge%20Cmte%20E.pdf>.
40. Ibid.
41. Interview, Sharalyn Jordan, 2010.
42. For more on the controversy surrounding the ban on QuAIA from Pride Toronto, see this open letter from the founders of Pride in 1981 <http://queersagainstapartheid.org/2010/05/27/open-letter-to-pride-toronto-from-founders-of-pride-in-1981/>.
43. Interview, Suhail Abualsameed, 2010.
44. Ibid.
45. Ibid.

Chapter 8: Where Do We Go From Here?

1. Paul Gallant, "The Honeymoon's Over: What's Next for the Gay Rights Movement?" *This Magazine*, September/October 2009.
2. "Our Mission," Queer Ontario, 2011 <http://queerontario.org/about-su>.
3. *Queers Made This: A Visual Archive of Queer Organizing in Montreal, 2005–2010*, QTeam Publishing, 2011.

ACKNOWLEDGEMENTS

Writing this book has been an enlightening and thoroughly fulfilling experience that would have never proved successful had it not been for a few dozen fabulous individuals.

First and foremost, I must extend my gratitude to everyone at Fernwood Publishing and most especially Jessica Antony and Wayne Antony for bestowing such an opportunity on me in the first place. Their enthusiasm for the project was really inspiring and kept me going through every stage of the process. Special thanks as well to my thoughtful and meticulous editor Ruth Bradley-St-Cyr and to Debbie Mathers, Brenda Conroy, John van der Woude and Beverley Rach for production.

I must also wholeheartedly thank the voices that guided me through that process by sharing their stories: Suhail AbualSameed, Brenda Cossman, Lynne Fernie, Sky Gilbert, Gerald Hannon, Gens Hellquist, Ross Higgins, Sean Horlor, Ed Jackson, Sharalyn Jordan, Ted Kerr, Wade King, Bev Lepischak, Stephen Lock, Elizabeth Massiah, Tim McCaskell, Robin Metcalfe, Chris Morrissey, Glen Murray, Lorna Murray, Robin Perelle, Steve Polyak, Ken Popert, Michael Phair, David Rayside, Michael Riordan, Dexter Roberts, Chad Smith, Chris Vogel, David Walberg, Thomas Waugh, Jeffrey White, Alan Wong, Kristyn Wong-Tam and Ryan Zeta-Hinds. These people all lent their time, knowledge and history to this book (even if it wasn't explicitly noted), and without them it would not have been possible. In that vein, I must too thank the authors listed throughout this book and the staff of the Canadian Gay and Lesbian Archives, who — with consistent charm — directed me to their invaluable work.

Finally, this book is indebted to the people who influenced and encouraged me in finding a place where taking on such a project was even possible: to *indieWIRE*, for giving me the time to write it; to Robert Carter, Michael Cobb, Scott Rayter, Leslie Regan Shade and Rae Staseson, for all being such extraordinary teachers; to Basil, Brad, Jenny, Mark, Matt, Paul, Shaun, Sophie and Toby, for being such affecting partners in queerness; to Michael, for being such a patient and loving partner in domesticity; and to the remarkable members of my immediate family, a quartet of queer activists in their own little way.